CUP OF LIFE

Lord of the world, he reigned alone
  While yet the universe was naught.
  When by his will all things were wrought,
Then first his sovran Name was known.

And when the All shall cease to be,
  In dread lone splendour he shall reign.
  He was, he is, he shall remain
In glorious eternity.

For he is one, no second shares
  His nature or his loneliness;
  Unending and beginningless,
All strength is his, all sway he bears.

He is the living God to save,
  My Rock while sorrow's toils endure,
  My banner and my stronghold sure,
The cup of life whene'er I crave.

I place my soul within his palm
  Before I sleep as when I wake,
  And though my body I forsake,
Rest in the Lord in fearless calm.

(This hymn, *Adon Olam* — 'Lord of the World' — is by the 11th-century Spanish-Jewish philosopher, Solomon ibn Gabirol, and comes near the beginning of the daily service in the synagogue; it also has a place in other parts of Jewish liturgy, for example at the close of the Sabbath morning service. It is a hymn universally chosen for all solemn state and memorial occasions, translated here by Israel Zangwill.)

CUP OF LIFE

A Short History of Post-biblical Judaism

Albert I. Polack and Joan Lawrence

LONDON
SPCK

First published 1976
SPCK
Holy Trinity Church
Marylebone Road
London NW1 4DU

Printed in Great Britain by
Unwin Brothers Limited, The Gresham Press,
Old Woking, Surrey

ISBN 0 281 02915 6

CONTENTS

ACKNOWLEDGEMENTS

Thanks are due to Vallentine, Mitchell & Co. Ltd for permission to quote copyright material from *Prelude to Dialogue* by Dr James Parkes, and to Routledge & Kegan Paul Ltd for permission to quote from *Judaism as Creed and Life* by Morris Joseph.

Biblical quotations are taken in general from the Revised Standard Version of the Bible, © 1946, 1952, and 1957 by the Division of Christian Education of the National Council of Churches of Christ in the United States of America, and are used by permission.

Quotations from the Authorized Daily Prayer Book of the United Hebrew Congregations of the British Empire (with a translation by S. Singer) are used by permission of the Singer's Prayer Book Publication Committee.

FOREWORD

I welcome the opportunity of writing a brief Foreword to this book, not only because it is an admirable instance of scholarly co-operation between a Christian and a Jew, but also because it fills a need which, so far as I know, has hitherto not been met. I refer to the need of a one-volume account of the history of post-Biblical Judaism suitable for use in colleges and schools. The field is a very big one, and I congratulate the authors on the way in which they have covered so much ground in a comparatively small space.

We who are Christians have much to be ashamed of as we consider the treatment meted out by 'Christians' to Jews down the centuries. It is a sorry story, and repentance is called for.

If, as I believe it will, the reading of this book leads to a better understanding of the history, the learning and the piety of a people to whom Christians must for ever be in debt, it will have achieved a very worthwhile purpose. I wish it well.

DONALD CANTUAR:

INTRODUCTION

This book is intended, primarily, for the non-Jewish reader, as well as for students of religious history generally. Its object is twofold: firstly, to correct the widely held view that, while Judaism expressed what was highest in man's thought and experience before the rise of Christianity, it had no subsequent development of any significance, becoming an obsolete, legalistic system devoid of further inspiration; secondly, to show that the post-biblical history of the Jewish people up to the present day throws an important light on history in general, and on European history in particular. For this is history with a difference. From the time of the Roman Emperor Hadrian until the Arab-Israel struggle, precipitated by the establishment of the State of Israel in 1948 — that is, for a period of nearly 2,000 years — we do not find Jews, as Jews, involved in wars or the responsibility of statehood. There are no kings or queens; no panoply of state; no upkeep of armed forces or of the administration of a nation; no economic, political or territorial history for which Jews were nationally accountable. It is the simple record of a people who, in the beginning, believed themselves to have been vouchsafed a divine vocation and a social responsibility. In each successive period we find the members of this extraordinary little community, whose only aristocracy was that of learning, seeking to discharge their responsibilities in a world which either denied or was unable to understand their vocation.

It follows, however, that the unique and concentrated experience of being always a minority group would inevitably exert a direct and sometimes decisive influence on the social, cultural and economic history of the nation among whom the Jewish people lived. This is especially evident in such important European movements as the Renaissance and the Reformation. But it is also true that their very existence within a nation provided a kind of touchstone by which that nation's civilization and stage of development could be judged. No balanced history, or religious history, of Europe can be written, therefore, without reference to the special contribution of the Jewish people.

A further motive for this book concerns the fact of our joint Jewish and Christian authorship. We feel that the presentation of post-biblical Jewish history must be free from anything in the nature of propaganda or apologetics, and be presented as objectively as possible. We make no claim to special scholarship or independent research, but have chosen rather to consult a large number of authorities. Among them, a special obligation is owed to the authors whose works are listed in the bibliography.

We hope that our co-operation over a number of years as, respectively, Education Officer and Publications Officer in the Council of Christians and Jews has enabled us to tell the story, as far as possible, without either bias or distortion.

Albert I. Polack
Joan Lawrence

DEVELOPMENT OF JEWISH WORSHIP AND FESTIVALS

The title of most history books clearly indicates the subject to be studied. No one, for instance, would be in doubt about the theme of a book entitled, say, *A Short History of England*, though there might be considerable diversity in its treatment. It might be written, as a history don once remarked, 'to the tune of *Rule, Britannia*', or it might be approached with the objectivity of a scientific historian. But whatever the approach, the basic theme would be the same: English history.

The meaning of 'post-biblical Judaism', however, is not altogether self-evident. The latest of the books of the Old Testament was probably the Book of Daniel, written somewhere about 165 B.C. (a Jew would speak of B.C.E., meaning 'before the common era', and, in place of A.D., would use C.E. or 'common era'). There followed a period of literary activity, the fruits of which were eventually collected together in what we now know as the Apocrypha and Pseudepigrapha (a later, similar work). With the exception of the first book of Maccabees, however, these writings contain little specifically historical information, though they throw some indirect light on Jewish life and thought during the two centuries preceding the Christian era. We therefore have to look to other sources than the so-called scriptural for information on this particular period. These include, for example, the works of the Jewish historian Flavius Josephus. The title 'post-biblical' Judaism, therefore, we take to mean the Jewish religious development which followed the completion of the Old Testament.

Legacy of the Old Testament
It was during this period, moreover, that the foundations of Judaism in something approaching its present form as an institutional religion were well and truly laid. The process began when those who returned to Palestine from the

Babylonian exile found that the remnant of the people who
had been left behind had freely intermarried with people of
non-Hebraic stock. This had resulted in a diluting of the
tradition derived from the Mosaic Law. The devout Jew
believed, then as now, that the Law (or Teaching — in Hebrew,
Torah) had been given to Moses on Mount Sinai. It was
buttressed by the inspired writings of the Prophets, with their
passion for righteousness and service of the one true God.
Enshrined in this teaching was a way of life which needed
for its preservation the rigid disciplines of separation from
the heathen and an ordered life of ritual and moral observances.
As early as 393 B.C., we find this process referred to as the
building of 'a fence around the Law'. It was instituted by
Ezra the Scribe, 'For Ezra had set his heart to study the law
of the Lord, and to do it, and to teach his statutes and ordinances in Israel' (Ezra 7.10). The impression made by Ezra
was one of overwhelming importance, so that it was said of
him to the people (Ezra 7.21): 'Whatever Ezra the priest, the
scribe of the law of the God of heaven, requires of you, be it
done with all diligence'.

Meaning of Torah

It is one of the interesting facts of history that the word
'Law' came to be used of something which was much wider
and more profound than the English word suggests. The
Hebrew word of which it purports to be a translation was
Torah, which in Jewish thought has really the basic meaning
of 'instruction'. This is used in two ways. One is concerned
with the written Law — that is, the Pentateuch or first five
books of the Bible; the second, and interrelated, with the
Oral Law, that stream of divine inspiration which runs through
the teaching of prophet, rabbi and sage throughout Jewish
history and up to the present day. Unfortunately, when the
Hebrew scriptures were translated into Greek, the word *nomos*,
with a much narrower meaning, was used for Torah, and a
good deal of misunderstanding of Judaism has resulted from
this difficulty about language.

It was the Oral Law, handed down by word of mouth
through the centuries from teacher to disciple and father to

son, that shaped the foundations of Judaism into an established religion. The chain of tradition, so beloved by the Jewish scholar, is described in the opening paragraph of the *Pirke Avot* ('Ethics of the Fathers'), a compilation from the Mishnah (see chapter 4) which embodies the quintessence of rabbinic wisdom and ethical and religious teaching: 'Moses received the Torah from Sinai, and he delivered it to Joshua, and Joshua to the Elders, and the Elders to the Prophets, and the Prophets delivered it to the men of the Great Synagogue.'

The origins of the Oral Law, then, lay in the Sinai revelation, in accordance with which the whole people of Israel dedicated themselves to the service of the one true God, proclaiming his message to mankind through the medium of both practice and precept: 'You shall be to me a kingdom of priests and a holy nation' (Exod. 19.6). In post-biblical times, there was a considerable change in the outlook of Jewish people towards the role which they were henceforth called upon to play. The phrase 'kingdom of priests' implies an outward rather than an inward look, a function rather than a racial or national group. To use two parallel phrases, they became *Am Berit*, a 'covenant people', and *Am Segulah*, the property of God, those who were consecrated to God and to his service. 'You shall be holy; for I the Lord your God am holy' (Lev. 19.2): this applied both to the individual Jew and to the people as a whole. That is why there is a conscious lack of distinction — applying equally to literature and the language of prayer — between corporate and personal Jewish life. But a priestly function, if it is to be carried out effectively, requires both training and discipline — a set of principles and rules which act as a constant reminder. This is exactly what the Torah and the Oral Law supplied.

Temple and Priesthood

In human society, ideas, teachings, customs or ways of life seldom survive without institutions; hence we have churches, parliaments, political parties, and so on, to give them positive expression. It was the same with the Torah or the Hebraic way of life. In earlier times, when the Jewish people were wandering in the wilderness of Sinai after the exodus from

Egypt, they had set up a tabernacle or tent of meeting as a focal point for their religious customs and ceremonies, and an elaborate system of animal sacrifice grew up around it which is described in great detail in the earlier books of the Bible, especially Exodus and Leviticus. Later, when they settled in the Promised Land and became a loose federation of twelve tribes, a religious centre was set up, first at Shechem and then at Shiloh, where the Ark of the Covenant (see the elaborate description in the twenty-fifth chapter of Exodus), originally placed in the Tabernacle, was subsequently housed. Still later, in the time of Solomon, a permanent Temple was built, and though at first this was little more than a royal chapel, it became the centre of Jewish worship, a living protest against the idolatry of surrounding peoples. In the course of time, when the people were widely scattered, it grew to be the focus of religious and national aspiration.

The bitterness caused by the destruction of the first Temple by Nebuchadnezzar in 586 B.C. is reflected in Lamentations. Following the exile, it was joyfully rebuilt (c. 516 B.C.), though Ezra described how 'many of the priests and Levites and heads of the fathers' houses, old men who had seen the first house, wept with a loud voice when they saw the foundation of this house being laid' (Ezra 3.12). Once more, during the last centuries B.C., it fell into decay and was rebuilt by Herod the Great in 20 B.C. This third Temple was the one with which Jesus was familiar, though we learn from the Gospel story that its outer courts were still incomplete (Mark 13.1; John 2.20). It is also the Temple from which is preserved today a famous portion of the surrounding wall — the *Kotel Maaravi*, traditionally known as the Wailing, now simply as the Western, Wall (see cover picture).

In the Temple, an elaborate system of worship and sacrifice was regularly carried out. There were processions accompanied by music, the singing of psalms by the Levitical choirs, as well as occasional dancing. On Sabbaths and Festivals additional sacrifices were offered and special songs (such as the Song of Moses in Deuteronomy) were sung. It must have been a breath-taking sight on these Holy Days, and it is not surprising to read these words of an early rabbi: 'He who has not taken part in the Tabernacles observances in Jerusalem has not lived.'

It is worth noting that a sacrifice in the Temple, where the beast had been the most perfect and unspotted animal a family could offer, then provided both a ceremonial meal and stored food for the particular family, and their friends, who had made the offering. Certain special delicacies were, by tradition, set aside for the Temple priests. The ceremonial meal was eaten in the vicinity of the Temple and must have had very much the character of the old-fashioned ceremonies of killing and roasting an ox in public. It is important to realize that these sacrifices were not the blood-stained, hysterical rites which western society has often assumed. The animals were offered in the first place for the blessing of God, and provided food for those who offered them. The tendency has been for westerners to feel aversion for rites which were perfectly comparable with our own: indeed, the attitude towards the sacrificed beast was almost certainly more humane than that involved in the slaughtering of an ox to feed merry-makers on the frozen Thames.

The ritual and upkeep of the Temple buildings and courts were in the hands of the priests, who claimed descent from Aaron, Moses' elder brother, and they were led by the so-called High Priest who was also the leading state official during the last centuries of the national state. They were divided into twenty-four panels or 'courses' who took over the duties in turn week by week. Below them were the Levites with their special functions, one section of which were the choristers (*Asaphites*) and another, porters or door-keepers (*Kohathites*). But in spite of this rather elaborate organization, the Temple worship was regarded as a combined corporate act of the whole people of Israel. Obviously, for geographical reasons, they could not 'assemble as one man'. But they satisfied their consciences, first by travelling to Jerusalem for the three Pilgrim Festivals, and secondly by sending representatives (as we do to Parliament) known as 'standing men' who, in twenty-five panels (as with the priests), took up their residence in Jerusalem for a week at a time and attended the Temple services.

Synagogue and School

With all this concentration on the Temple in Jerusalem and
its priesthood and elaborate sacrificial system, the religion
of the Jews might well have disappeared when the city was
captured by the Romans under Titus in A.D. 70 and its
Temple was finally destroyed. For not only was this the end
of the Jewish state — that is, of the political existence of the
Jews as a nation — as well as of its priestly administration,
but it seemed that the cultural and spiritual centre of Jewish
life and thought was gone for ever. The fact that Judaism
survived these disasters and has lasted right up to the present
day is, perhaps, one of the miracles of history. It can, however,
be accounted for if we try to examine once more the real
meaning of Torah and realize that this was basically a spiritual
legacy independent of political states, priestly officials and
national shrines — though not, of course, independent of
institutions. Judaism survived because, as we have seen, the
Torah endowed the whole Jewish people with a priestly function which could be carried out in any conditions and in any
part of the world.

That is why the religion held its ground at the time of the
deportations six centuries before the final overthrow of
Jerusalem, when Jews were carried captive to distant parts
of Babylon and later of the Persian Empire. As we know,
both from the later prophetic writings (for instance, the books
of Jeremiah, Ezekiel and the second Isaiah), as well as from
such semi-historical, semi-fictional books as Esther and Daniel,
an intense religious life developed among the little Jewish
communities scattered about the lands of their captivity. It
was here that the institution known as the Synagogue (a
Greek word meaning 'assembly') took shape. Originally the
place of 'coming together', it became for most Jews the
local centre of public worship. And this — inevitably
institutionalized — it has remained ever since.

The Synagogue became both a House of Assembly (*Beth
Ha-Keneset*) and a House of Prayer (*Beth Tephillah*). It was
here, week by week and day by day, that the little groups of
Jewish deportees directed their thoughts to God, sought
consolation for their misfortunes, conducted their religious

practices, and even in some cases provided accommodation for the traveller, in accordance with the principles and injunctions of the Torah. Even in exile, they turned in prayer to Jerusalem, still the focal point of their emotions, and this spirit is beautifully expressed in one of the post-Exilic Psalms: 'If I forget you, O Jerusalem, let my right hand wither!' (Ps. 137.5). To this day, synagogues in western countries are built with the Ark facing an easterly direction. This Ark is a closet or compartment in which the sacred Scrolls of the Law are housed. Like the altar or sanctuary of a church, the Ark is the focus of attention. In large synagogues, it is highly decorated and its doors are covered with richly embroidered velvet curtains.

The Scrolls themselves are of parchment, still written by hand, in accordance with long-established tradition. They are elaborately wrapped in velvet mantles and decorated with silver ornaments. These include silver finials, decorated with silver bells, whose tinkling as the Scroll is removed from the Ark and carried around the Synagogue symbolizes the joy of the worshippers in the Law of the Lord. Other decorations are a silver breastplate, and a silver pointer to enable the reader to follow the text more easily. No apparel can be too precious for this priceless treasure of the Divine Word.

The Synagogue was also a House of Learning (*Beth Ha-Midrash*). The love of study has always been a characteristic of the Jewish people, but it was religiously based and stemmed from a deep-seated belief that 'the fear of the Lord is the beginning of wisdom'. It differed from the Greek approach to learning, which was less circumscribed and included all kinds of knowledge in a spirit which today we would call scientific. Not that the Hebrew schools ruled out so-called secular subjects — the rabbis placed a good deal of stress on vocational and technical training — but the main incentive for the training of the human mind was, in Hebraic thought, always a greater understanding of God and his ways. In later times the school became a separate institution and played as important a part in Jewish life and practice as the Synagogue itself. The *Beth Ha-Midrash*, the centre for higher rabbinic study, was generally in close proximity to the

synagogue. It has to be distinguished from the primary
school, the *Beth Ha-Sepher* ('House of the Book'), or, more
popularly, the *Heder*. This system was the basis of subsequent
Jewish educational organization; in the Middle Ages and
ghetto periods, there was universal and generally free Jewish
education, and an illiterate male was seldom encountered in
the mediaeval community. In the small local communities
characteristic of this period, primary education was generally
in the hands either of the father or of a professional elementary teacher who might at the same time be one of the
communal functionaries or a scribe or copyist. Advanced
instruction in the Talmud (see chapter 4) would be volunteered
as a meritorious deed by learned householders. Adults would
continue throughout their lives to participate in study-groups,
almost as their sole diversion. In larger communities education
was more formally and elaborately organized. The ritual of
the Synagogue was less spectacular than that of the Temple
and consisted largely of prayers, readings from the sacred
scriptures and interpretations — or what today we would call
a sermon.

The Hebrew Bible consists of twenty-four books, divided
into three groups: the Law (or Torah), formed of the first
five books, from Genesis to Deuteronomy; the Prophets
(Isaiah, Jeremiah, Ezekiel, and so on); the Writings, a word
used to describe poetical and semi-philosophical books such
as the Psalms, Job, Ecclesiastes, Lamentations and the Song
of Songs. In the time of Ezra, there was probably little more
in the service than a reading from the Law, but later there
were two lessons (as in church services), one drawn from the
Pentateuch, the other from the Prophets or from the Writings.
For two reasons, the sermon (or *Derush*) became more and
more important as time went on: partly because the average,
simple member of the congregation could not understand the
lesson unexplained, and partly because, while scriptures and
prayers remained in Hebrew, the bulk of the people had
begun to use Aramaic — picked up during captivity — and
consequently no longer understood Hebrew. As the Jews
became still more widely scattered, this exposition was even
more necessary, for they came increasingly to speak the

language of the people among whom they lived — Greek, Latin and Arabic. In later times, they adopted the languages of modern peoples such as German and French, together with what was to become the *lingua franca* of Eastern European Jewry in particular: Yiddish. This was a form of German, written in Hebrew characters, with a considerable admixture of words and expressions deriving from Hebrew and from other tongues spoken by Jews in earlier centuries.

The Septuagint

Of all the scattered Jewish communities that grew up outside the Holy Land during the last pre-Christian centuries, perhaps the most important from a religious point of view was that at Alexandria, where of course the language was Greek. Since here, as elsewhere, the congregations no longer understood Hebrew, it became necessary for the scriptures to be read in Greek at the synagogues. The story of how they came to be translated into Greek tells how seventy-two scholars were all shut into different cells, yet finished simultaneously and produced identical versions. 'Would such agreement have been possible', wrote a modern Anglo-Jewish historian, 'if they had all worked together?'

This Greek version of the Bible became known in the Latin-speaking western world as the Septuagint (Latin, *septuaginta*: 70), and remained the Christian form of the Old Testament until Jerome's Latin translation, the Vulgate, was adopted by the Church early in the fourth century A D. Biblical scholars have always made full use of this version as a basis for comparison with doubtful passages in the Hebrew text. Indeed, where the best of the surviving Hebrew texts contain difficult and obscure passages, the Septuagint, based upon earlier and more accurate texts, seems likely to have retained more exactly the sense and feeling of the original. It was by methods such as these that Judaism, while becoming an established religion, retained sufficient flexibility to cater for the religious needs of a widely scattered people and to become for all time something greater and more inspiring than a national cult.

The Rabbi

So it came about that in the post-biblical development of Judaism the names of kings and priests gradually gave place to those of scholars and religious teachers. The Hebrew word for them was rabbi (teacher) and it was the rabbi who has shaped the course of Jewish learning, practice and belief from somewhere about the second century B.C. right up to the present day.

This formidable task meant nothing less than applying the sacred principles of the Torah to the lives and needs of widely dispersed groups in changing political systems and social conditions. To do this, the rabbis built on the work of the scribes, of whom Ezra was the first, whose task it had been to copy the sacred books by hand, edit and amend them where necessary, so that an acceptable version, or canon, could be used by synagogues and schools all over the world. It is largely to their scholarship that we owe the splendid Hebrew text of the Old Testament in use in its original or in a translated form among the three great monotheistic religions today.

But the rabbi, in his task of teaching, had to interpret, expound and adapt. The Law, that is the written Law, was of very ancient origin and bore traces of many different authors and widely separated periods. It contained a complex series of prescribed rules ranging from the minutest regulations about ceremonies and sacrifices to the inculcation of the highest moral and social principles and codes of behaviour. According to the rabbis, who loved figures and statistics, it contained no less than 613 precepts, of which 365 were positive and 248 negative. Much analytical and dialectical skill was required to make this code fit in with the life of a Jew in, say, the European countries during the Middle Ages or the scientific age of today. It is interesting to note, for instance, how various teachers have compressed the 613 precepts down to ten, and to two, and to one. The ten precepts, of course, are the Ten Commandments. The two are the two great sayings, 'Thou shalt love the Lord thy God' and 'Thou shalt love thy neighbour as thyself'. The single precept has frequently been told in an anecdote about the great sage,

Hillel: how a young man, seeking to catch out the teacher, asked to be taught all the Law while he stood on one foot (i.e., to put it in a nutshell), and how he received the reply: 'What is hateful to thee, do not do unto thy fellow man; this is the whole Law; the rest is commentary.'

The dilemma of making a code fit into ordinary life is one which always faces those who believe in divine revelation: how to recognize that God made his will known to a particular person or group at a particular moment in history, and also to recognize the desirability of progress and change. But the rabbis were essentially practical, and they met the dilemma in their own unique and involved fashion. A good example of the methods they employed was the legal fiction (*prosbul*) of Rabbi Hillel, who lived shortly before the time of Christ. The people of his day were faced with an impossible law, called the Law of Release (Deut. 15.1-18) which stated that all debts were remitted or cancelled every seventh year. If this law were in force today, we can imagine how everybody would borrow large sums of money in the sixth year with no thought of repayment! It was, in fact, a well-intentioned but quite impracticable piece of legislation. Hillel interpreted the law as meaning that a debt could be reclaimed at any time except during the Year of Release, which meant that no borrower could keep his loan in perpetuity.

Through devices of this kind, many primitive or out-of-date laws were quietly superseded, without being deleted from the statute book. The *lex talionis*, for example ('an eye for an eye, a tooth for a tooth'), was never applied in the literal sense but was interpreted in terms of a financial fine or compensation suited to a particular injury. Incidentally, this had always been a comparatively humane law, signifying (in the days of personal family vendettas) *not more than* a punishment which fitted the crime.

Without the kind of adaptation reflected in these devices, the Jewish people could not have survived. For instance, their laws forbade them to fight on the Sabbath, but the rabbis argued that the Torah, which included the regulations about Sabbath rest based on the Fourth Commandment, was given to Israel for life and not for death: 'the Sabbath was made

for man, not man for the Sabbath.' An example of this can
be seen in the New Testament, in the story of the man with
the withered hand (Mark 3.1-4) which Jesus healed with the
words: 'Is it lawful on the sabbath to do good or to do harm,
to save life or to kill?' Such instances were, of course, the
exceptions, not the rule, and in the main the Jews of those
times — and right through history — clung to the actual letter
of their code as well as to the spirit with a loyalty which could
only spring from deep reverence and love.

Religious Customs

As it was the rabbinic tradition that kept Judaism alive after
the fall of the Temple, so also it was this tradition which
shaped some of the customs and ceremonies through which
the religion was given practical expression. Judaism has never
had any creed or formal declaration of faith, but from its
earliest days great importance was attached to what is called
the *Shema* — verses from the sixth chapter of Deuteronomy
(vv.4-9) proclaiming God's unity and man's duty towards
him:

> Hear, O Israel:
> The Lord our God is one Lord;
> and you shall love the Lord your God with all your heart,
> and with all your soul,
> and with all your might.
> And these words which I command you this day
> shall be upon your heart;
> and you shall teach them diligently to your children,
> and shall talk of them when you sit in your house,
> and when you walk by the way,
> and when you lie down,
> and when you rise.
> And you shall bind them as a sign upon your hand,
> and they shall be as frontlets between your eyes.
> And you shall write them on the doorposts of your house
> and on your gates.

With these verses were associated two other passages, one
from the eleventh chapter of Deuteronomy (vv.13-21), the

other from the fifteenth chapter of Numbers (vv. 37-41). Though it was the spirit of the verses that really mattered, the language being largely metaphorical, yet they have been given a literal interpretation by Jews throughout the ages. For example, a small case called a *Mezuzah* (Hebrew: 'doorpost'), which contained the Deuteronomic passages, was fixed on the right doorpost of a Jewish home, to become a source of inspiration to the devout Jew in his ordinary, everyday life and to emphasize the sanctity of the family.

During morning prayers, every male member of the community put on phylacteries (or, *Tephillin*, from 'prayer'), consisting of two small leather cases containing these same words. The phylacteries were bound round his forehead and left arm, opposite the heart, as a daily reminder that the words should be in his mind and heart.

Another passage of the *Shema* (Num. 15.38-9), commands the wearing of a fringe of blue and white on his outer garment, and this was the origin of the *Tallit* (surplice or shawl) still worn by all male members of a congregation at their Sabbath and Festival services.

There are other reminders, too, that the whole of life was to be consecrated to the service of God. Eight days after birth, a Jewish boy was initiated into the covenant by circumcision. According to tradition, the rite is traced back to Abraham (R.V. Gen. 17.10ff.):

This is my covenant, which ye shall keep, between me and you and thy seed after thee: every male among you shall be circumcized. And ye shall be circumcized in the flesh of your foreskin; and it shall be a token of a covenant betwixt me and you. And he that is eight days old shall be circumcized among you; every male throughout your generations. . . And the uncircumcized male who is not circumcized in the flesh of his foreskin, that soul shall be cut off from his people; he hath broken my covenant.

The word 'soul' gives some indication of the spiritual significance of circumcision. To be a member of the covenant meant to make a personal response which touched every aspect of daily life, and the application of a physical event, as symbol, to a spiritual act is seen (Deut. 10.16) when, as a sign of repentance, Israel is called to 'circumcise therefore the foreskin of your heart, and be no longer stubborn.'

Throughout the whole of life, following circumcision, there were special religious ceremonies: confirmation (called *Bar Mitzvah*, or 'son of the commandment', for boys, and *Bat Mitzvah*, for girls), marriage, and at death. Many of the ordinary activities of the day (for instance, the washing of hands before a meal) were sanctified by special prayers.

Perhaps the oldest and most important of prayers, still recited in synagogues today all over the world, is the *Shemoneh Esreh*, or Eighteen Benedictions, commonly called the *Amidah* (from *Amad*, to stand) because the worshippers recite them in a standing position facing the Ark. Some parts of these eighteen petitions can be traced back as far as the fourth century B.C., while the prayer as a whole achieved its present form somewhere around the year A.D. 100. The petitions begin with the individual's spiritual needs: for understanding, repentance and forgiveness. It is not until he has prayed for these that he goes on to pray for deliverance from affliction, for healing and for the fruits of the earth. The *Amidah* ends with an impressive act of thanksgiving for the unfailing mercies of God.

Festivals

There were three major festivals in the Jewish religious year for which all males were expected to make the journey to Jerusalem 'to offer the customary sacrifice in the Temple'. To use the language of Deuteronomy (16.16):

Three times a year all your males shall appear before the Lord your God at the place which he will choose: at the feast of unleavened bread, at the feast of weeks, at the feast of booths. They shall not appear before the Lord empty-handed; every man shall give as he is able, according to the blessing of the Lord your God which he has given you.

Originally, and naturally, linked with important phases of the agricultural year, these festivals came also to have an important national significance. The Festival of Passover commemorates the Exodus from Egypt; it took place in the spring, when in the land of Canaan the barley was already ripe. The two other festivals were Pentecost and Tabernacles, the wheat and fruit harvest festivals respectively, the first celebrated in midsummer, and the second in the early autumn.

Besides these joyous festivals and a monthly act of rejoicing at the new moon (*Rosh Hodesh*), there were two solemn observances, New Year (*Rosh Ha-Shanah*) and the Day of Atonement (*Yom Kippur*). The religious year began in the autumn with the seventh month (*Tishri*) and was ushered in with a period directed to self-examination and spiritual analysis, and on New Year a trumpet-call was sounded on a ram's horn (*Shofar*) to summon the people to battle — not against other people but against their own failings and sins. This period of repentance (*Teshuvah*, literally, a 'return') ended with the Day of Atonement, when the Israelite was commanded to 'afflict his soul' — interpreted to mean abstention from food and drink for one entire day. Atonement, or the reconciliation with his fellow men, was a prelude to atonement with God.

The most typical — and, indeed, most important — of all the Jewish institutions was that of the Sabbath, the day of rest at the end of each week. Other peoples could not understand this passion for compulsory rest, and a Roman poet, Juvenal, thought it must be due to a love of idleness. But, for the Jew, it expressed all his love of God who, he believed, had rested on the seventh day after the work of creation and who commanded his creature to 'call the Sabbath a delight', to put aside all worldly cares and occupations and devote himself to prayer and spiritual joy.

Universalism and Messianic Hopes

At about the period when Judaism became an established religion for a particular people, there was also among a section of Jewish writers and thinkers a growing emphasis on the universal implications of their vocation. The prophets had

already proclaimed in their sublime language that the whole
earth belonged to God, and had addressed to any Jews who
might think in terms of privilege or exclusiveness such
admonitions as 'Are you not like the Ethiopians to me?'
(Amos 9.7). This universalism was especially stressed in such
late books of the Old Testament as Ruth and Jonah. The
universal moral law had always been regarded by Jewish
teachers as more important than the ceremonial imposed on
a particular group, and they came to formulate a code, binding
on all mankind, called the Noachic Laws. These were seven
injunctions traditionally given to Noah and deriving from the
early chapters of Genesis (e.g. 9.4-7). They consisted of pro-
hibitions against blasphemy, idolatry, sexual immorality,
murder, robbery, an injunction against eating a portion of a
living animal, and an injunction concerning the administration
of justice. This occured centuries before the revelation to
Israel on Mount Sinai.

Certain new conceptions about the future of the whole
human race began to appear, first in the later prophetic
books and then in the post-biblical literature called Apocrypha and Pseudepigrapha. The Greek word 'apocalyptic' means,
quite simply, 'uncovering the future'. It looked to a time
when man would lead the perfect life as his creator intended,
when there would be an end to all strife and cruelty and
oppression and the 'reign of peace and love would be established on earth'. It also understood that man, of himself,
was unable to achieve this perfect state, that God was involved
in the establishment of this reign of peace, and that, when
human effort failed, God would intervene.

There were different notions as to how this could be
brought about. One set of ideas centred around the figure of
a so-called Messiah ('anointed servant'), a descendant of the
House of David, who would lead the scattered Israelites back
to the Holy Land and at the same time redeem all the nations
of the world so that 'the earth shall be full of the knowledge
of the Lord as the waters cover the sea' (Isa. 11.9). Another
was that of redemption through suffering; either by the
suffering of an individual or of the whole people of Israel.
In either case the 'suffering servant' (Isa. 53) was to carry

on his shoulders the sins of mankind and through pain and sacrifice win salvation for all men.

A third idea, which had a great influence on the rise of the new religion, Christianity, was that God himself would intervene in human history and miraculously send 'The Son of Man' — a title found in Jewish apocalyptic literature (as well as in the New Testament where it referred to Jesus) in order to bring his kingdom into the world of men. This idea was expressed in a highly poetic passage from a book of the first century B.C., *The Testaments of the Twelve Patriarchs*:

> Then shall the Lord raise up a new priest
> and to him all the words of the Lord shall be revealed;
> . . . And his star shall arise in Heaven as of a king
> Lighting up the light of knowledge as the sun the day . . .
> And there shall none succeed him for all generations for ever,
> And in his priesthood the gentiles shall be multiplied in
>   knowledge upon the earth,
> And enlightened through the grace of the Lord.
>
> *Testament of Levi 18.2-9*

This concept of a supernatural figure did not find much support in the main stream of Jewish thinking, though it played a large part in the outlook of Judaism's great daughter religion, Christianity. In so far as Judaism dwelt on the coming of 'the kingdom', it was to be ushered in by a human Messiah without any break in the historical process. More important still, ever since Judaism became an established religion, the whole Jewish people regarded themselves as having to carry out this kind of Messianic function in hastening on the time when, in the words of *Alenu*, the concluding prayer of synagogue services, 'the world will be perfected under the kingdom of the Almighty and all the children of flesh will call upon thy name.'

2

GREEK INFLUENCE AND THE SUPPRESSION OF JUDAISM

Alexander's Conquests

One of the most serious challenges which post-biblical Judaism had to face in its earliest years came largely as the result of a historical event of world-wide significance. In the year 333 B.C., through his victory over the Persians, Alexander the Great became master of the whole eastern world. This remarkable man, though a Macedonian by birth, had, during his childhood, come under the influence of two Greek tutors. One of them was Lysimachus of Acarnania, who had implanted in him a love of the Homeric poems; the other, who supervised his education, was the philosopher Aristotle, one of the world's supreme intellects. Alexander, as a result of his youthful studies, conceived when he grew up the tremendous idea of turning the whole world into one vast city-state. In pursuit of this ideal — armed, in a military sense, with the Macedonian phalanx and, in the spiritual, with the cultural ideals of Hellas — he pushed his conquests as far east as the River Indus, subduing both Persia and India in the process.

Next, he turned his attention to Egypt, which submitted to him without a struggle, and there are several stories, some of them legendary, about his passage through the little country of Palestine and his contacts with the Hebrews. One is that he was met by the High Priest, Jaddua, who offered him the submission of his people and so prevented his marching on Jerusalem. Another, recorded by Josephus, was that he offered a sacrifice in the Temple 'according to the direction of the High Priest'. In any case, it seems certain that he was the most merciful and tolerant of Israel's conquerors, and this may have had its effect on the confrontations which then took place between the systems of thought and culture known respectively as Hebraism and Hellenism.

Greek Influences

Most scholars agree that Greek ideas had in fact infiltrated
Hebrew thought even before this, and some have gone so far
as to assert that Homer and the Bible both sprang from a
common literary heritage which derives from the period of the
ancient Babylonian creation myth, the Gilgamesh Epic
(*c.* 3,000 B.C.). But this is speculation. What is perhaps more
remarkable about the biblical period is that there was so little
communication between the two civilizations, although the
great Athenian dramatists, philosophers and historians, such
as Aeschylus, Plato, Aristotle and Thucydides, were all writing
and teaching during the period between the second Isaiah and
Daniel — that is, from about 540 to 300 B.C.

This is not to say, however, that Greek ideas and thought
had no influence on the biblical writers of this period. On the
contrary, what is called the Wisdom literature (a term applied
to particular biblical books such as Proverbs, Job, Ecclesiastes
and others, of which wisdom was the central theme) shows
that certain Greek concepts and patterns of thought had
penetrated into the Hebraic world. After Alexander's conquest, this confrontation became even more spectacular.
Greek habits and modes of life began to affect the culture of
Jewish people in the very centres of Hebraism, and in this
fashion a way of life which rested on simplicity, purity and
holiness came face to face with an intellectual, aesthetic and
highly cultivated form of paganism.

The result was not all loss. The Jews, like other ancient
peoples (and, indeed, modern ones, too), were liable to
'wrap themselves in their own virtue' and, particularly since
the separatist movement at the time of Ezra and the drawing
of 'a fence round the law', had tended to live in an ivory
tower. The advent of the Greeks had the effect of disturbing
this isolationism and led indirectly to a recognition of other
non-Hebraic insights. Its immediate benefits can be seen in
the Greek translation of the Bible, the Septuagint, in the
Apocryphal writings, and in the works of Josephus and the
Alexandrian Jewish philosopher, Philo.

There was, however, a debit side. It was not the pure ray of
Hellenic thought that swept over Palestine in the wake of

Alexander's armies and those of his successors. The culture they brought was Hellenistic rather than Hellenic, a blend of oriental magnificence, ruthlessness and lust for power, with the sensual and often licentious cult associated with the gymnasium and temples of the Olympic deities. *'In Tiberim defluxit Orontes'*, bewailed the Roman satiric poet, Juvenal: or, as we might paraphrase it, 'the pure Roman stream has been defiled by the dregs of the East.'

To this culture, many of the leading Jewish families in Palestine fell prey during the early post-biblical period. It became a fashion among them to admire everything Greek, to assume Greek names, put on Greek clothes and adopt the Greek language, customs and architecture. Priests were not immune from the new craze, and when Jason became High Priest in 175 B.C., he did his best to turn Jerusalem into a Greek city where, within actual sight of the Temple, a Greek gymnasium was erected.

Suppression of Judaism under Antiochus

This process of assimilation might have gone on undisturbed and led to a serious and permanent weakening of Judaism had not an event occurred which produced a powerful reaction and reassertion of Hebraic values. Ten years after his victory over the Persians, Alexander the Great died, leaving his newly won empire to be divided among his generals. A period of great confusion followed, during which the little country of Palestine became a bone of contention between two of Alexander's surviving generals, Seleucus and Ptolemy, the former becoming ruler of Babylon and Syria, the latter of Egypt. It was during the ensuing period that serious internal dissension broke out amongst the Jews of Palestine, particularly as to the function and authority of the High Priest. Ever since the rediscovery in the Temple of a 'book of the Law' (thought by many scholars to have been Deuteronomy) during the reign of Josiah, the Jews had cherished the concept of a priestly ruler who would administer the state in accordance with theocratic principles. This dream almost came true in the person of the High Priest Simon the Just — though opinions differ as to whether there were two Simons or only one who merited this title. It is accepted by some that the following passage from the Apocrypha (Ecclus. 50.1-11) shows the impression Simon the Just made on his contemporaries:

... Simon the high priest, son of Onias,
who in his life repaired the house,
and in his time fortified the temple.

.   .   .

He considered how to save his people from ruin,
and fortified the city to withstand a siege.
How glorious he was when the people gathered round him
as he came out of the inner sanctuary!
Like the morning star among the clouds,

.   .   .

When he put on his glorious robe and clothed himself with
superb perfection and went up to the holy altar,
he made the court of the sanctuary glorious.

As we have seen, the office fell later into the hands of the Hellenists such as Jason, but the whole situation was changed when a member of the Seleucid dynasty, Antiochus IV (175-163 B.C.), wrenched Palestine from the Egyptian Ptolemies and forcibly intervened in the religious affairs of the country. In 169 B.C., Antiochus determined to put an end to the anti-Hellenist movement by suppressing the practice of Judaism and imposing a Hellenic culture on the Jewish people. Not only did his invading army carry out a campaign of plunder and brutality, but he compelled pious Jews to worship idols and eat the forbidden swine's flesh. On one occasion, a mother and her seven children were successively butchered in front of the governor for refusing to bow down to an image. Here is this woman's exhortation to her seventh child:

My son, have pity on me. I carried you nine months in my womb, and nursed you for three years, and have reared you and brought you up to this point in your life, and have taken care of you. . . . Do not fear this butcher, but prove worthy of your brothers. Accept death, so that in God's mercy I may get you back again with your brothers.
(2 Macc. 7.27,29)

Finally, the Temple itself was desecrated and an idol erected in the sacred precinct.

Maccabean Revolt

Resistance to these atrocities committed by Antiochus and his Hellenizing confederates finally arose from the villages outside Jerusalem. It came to a head when a priest called Mattathias pulled down an altar at Modin and slew both the officer in charge and a fellow Jew who was about to offer a sacrifice on it. This was followed up, according to the account in the Apocrypha, by Mattathias crying aloud: 'Even if all the nations that live under the rule of the king obey him departing each one from the religion of his fathers, yet I and my sons and my brothers will live by the covenant of our fathers. Far be it from us to desert the law and the ordinances' (1 Macc. 2.19-21). He then withdrew to the mountains with his five sons (called 'the Maccabees', a term which may mean 'hammer' or is possibly an acrostic of the biblical verse 'Who is like unto thee among the Gods?'). Here he called upon all faithful Jews to join him and set up the banner of revolt — one of the first blows in history struck for religious freedom. After a number of victories, Judah the Maccabee (famous even today as the subject of one of Handel's oratorios), who had become leader of the insurgents after his father's death in 166 B.C., entered Jerusalem and reconsecrated the Temple. The festival of *Hanukkah* ('dedication') is still kept in Jewish homes and synagogues today in memory of this great deliverance and is marked by the lighting of candles on an eight-branch candlestick (Hebrew: *'Menorah'*), because it was said that the tiny amount of consecrated oil found undefiled in the Temple lasted miraculously for eight days until further supplies were prepared.

After the death of Judah in 160 B.C., still fighting bravely to free his country from the foreign yoke, the Hasmonean dynasty was founded by Simon, the last surviving son of Mattathias. His leadership was marked by a period of peace and tranquillity, a good description of which is found in the literature of the period:

They tilled their land in peace;
the ground gave its increase,
and the trees of the plains their fruit.
Old men sat in the streets;
they all talked together of good things;
and the youths donned the glories and garments of war.
He supplied the cities with food,
and furnished them with the means of defense,
till his renown spread to the ends of the earth.
He established peace in the land,
and Israel rejoiced with great joy.
Each man sat under his vine and his fig tree,
and there was none to make them afraid.
No one was left in the land to fight them,
and the kings were crushed in those days.
He strengthened all the humble of his people;
he sought out the law,
and did away with every lawless and wicked man.
He made the sanctuary glorious,
and added to the vessels of the sanctuary.

(1 Macc. 2.19-21)

Hasmonean Dynasty
One of the saddest features of history is the degeneracy which
sets in when a religious or spiritual movement becomes
identified with power politics and secular authority. The
best-known examples are perhaps to be found in the early
Islamic Caliphate, in the Crusades and in the Spanish Inquisition initiated by the mediaeval Church, but their prototype
is to be found in the deterioration which set in during the
later years of the Hasmonean dynasty.

There was an immediate increase of Jewish power when
Simon's son, John Hyrcanus, became ruler and started to
conquer the neighbouring countries, and with it came a weakening of the principles of Torah. Foreign peoples such as the
Edomites were forcibly converted to Judaism, and the later
Hasmoneans started to imitate the very Hellenistic despots
whom the Maccabean movement had so bravely defied,
surrounding themselves with all the pomp and panoply of an

oriental throne and employing foreign mercenaries. The area under Jewish control at this period was larger than at any time in their history, including that of Solomon.

Jewish ideology, however, does not easily conform to secular patterns of thought, and the power mechanism of this new age held within it a core which was bound to lead to its own disruption. This was the hard core of Hebraism, faithfulness to which gave birth to a new movement led by the Hasidim (not to be confused with the better-known Hasidic movement of the eighteenth century) who, known as the 'faithful' or the 'pious', resurrected the ancient prophetic cry, 'Not by might nor by power, but by my spirit, saith the Lord of Hosts'. As a result of the ideological conflict that now arose between this movement and the upholders of the Hasmonean dynasty, an internal paralysis set in, and the state lost its solidarity and became an easy prey to any would-be intruder or conqueror.

3

ROMAN OCCUPATION AND THE RISE
OF CHRISTIANITY

Judaea: a Roman Province

The tense situation which had arisen as the result of the
oppressive policy of the later Hasmoneans, particularly
Alexander Jannaeus, came to a head after his death when
his two sons, John Hyrcanus (the younger) and Aristobulus,
were contending for the throne — which meant, in this secular
age, the High Priesthood as well. The position was further
complicated by the intervention of Antipater, who, himself
not an Edomite, was ruler of Idumaea, the Edomite kingdom,
and son of the man who had been appointed its first ruler by
Jannaeus. Fearing the power of the more ambitious brother,
Aristobulus, he began giving active support to Hyrcanus.

But at this time (*c.* 66 B.C.), the Roman general, Pompey,
was extending Roman domination in the East and, when he
learnt of the internal squabbles going on in Palestine, he
decided that this was a golden opportunity for applying the
old Roman principle of 'divide and rule'. Both sides offered
bribes for his support, and Aristobulus, the higher bidder,
succeeded in gaining it. Pompey, however, decided to enter
the country. On the whole, he behaved with typical Roman
moderation, though it is said that he entered the holy of
holies in the Temple, an act forbidden to anyone except the
High Priest on the Day of Atonement. He appointed Hyrcanus
as High Priest and Ethnarch (Greek: 'Ruler of a people'),
since he found Aristobulus completely untrustworthy. The
country was in fact divided into four ethnarchies, Judaea,
Galilee, Idumaea, Peraea, each with its own ruler, nominated
by Rome. Samaria and the coastline were at this time detached
from the rest.

Unfortunately, however, for the Jews, it was the ruler of
Idumaea, Antipater, who became the virtual nominee of
Rome. He and his son, the second Antipater, as well as his
grandson, Herod the Great, exercised a foreign and therefore
much-hated domination over the Jewish people during the

next sixty years. In spite of the fact that Herod, during his long reign, showed a certain amount of statesmanship — even, in order to gain Jewish popularity, rebuilding the Temple — he could never gain their genuine support. Eventually, when one of Herod's three sons, Archelaus, was appointed ruler of Judaea, a Jewish deputation went to Rome asking that their country might come under direct Roman rule. This led to the incorporation of Judaea into the provincial system, so that henceforth it was governed by Roman procurators. The fifth of these was Pontius Pilate, to whom we shall presently return.

Internal Freedom

Rome was without doubt the most tolerant of ancient peoples. Though some of her provincial governors, such as the notorious Verres of Sicily, were cruel and extortionate men, her policy in general was to allow the judicial and cultural practices of her subjects to continue unimpeded, provided that her political leadership was accepted without question. Her aim, in Virgil's words, was *'pacis imponere morem'*: to establish the custom of peace. Thus in Judaea, in spite of the exactions of the much-hated *publicani* or 'tax-gatherers' and the poverty from which certain sections of the people suffered as the result of a succession of wars, industry and trade flourished throughout a large part of the country. Respect for manual labour was inculcated by the rabbis, who themselves earned their living as craftsmen and, like the Greek 'pedagogue', taught without receiving any financial remuneration. In fact, the aristocracy in Judaism, since the close of the monarchic and priestly period, has never been one of wealth or political power, but of learning. But even teachers have to live, whence that superb rabbinic aphorism: 'When a man teaches his son no trade, it is as if he taught him highway robbery!'

The religious life of the people also went on unhampered during the period of Roman government. This was based partly on the Temple worship (until A.D. 70), with its hierarchy, its elaborate routine of prayer and sacrifice, and its Levitical choirs for which the Psalms had been composed.

These latter were organized choirs of Levites, participating in the Temple service; they were descendants of the tribe of Levi, consecrated to serve in the cult of the Tabernacle and to instruct the people. Religious life under Rome was also based partly on the Synagogue (see p. 8), the home and house of learning. The judicial system, too, with its courts of law (*Beth Din*, in Hebrew, *Sanhedrin* in Greek), continued without interference from the imperial power — though a political court was set up by the governor of Judaea to act in cases of subversive activity. It was probably this court which was responsible for the arrest and preliminary trial of Jesus.

The Sects
One of the interesting features of Jewish history is that it never conformed to conventional patterns. This can be seen in the peculiar blend of religious and political concepts which has always shaped the destiny of the Jewish people. Thus, during the Roman occupation, a number of groups emerged, partly political, partly religious. Four of these assumed special importance. They were called respectively Pharisees, Sadducees, Essenes, and Zealots.

The Pharisees. There is some division of opinion among scholars about the meaning of the word Pharisee, as the Hebrew root *'parush'* from which it is derived means both 'to separate' and 'to expound'. It is true that this sect laid great emphasis on ritual cleanliness and so separated, or set themselves apart, from those they considered unclean. Thus St Paul, who proudly claimed to be a 'Pharisee of the Pharisees', exhorted the Christians in Corinth to separate themselves from the pagan society in which they had been brought up. 'Come out from them', he wrote (2 Cor. 6.17) 'and be separate'.

Yet it can also be said that, as so often happens with those who aspire to piety, some of them became what we should call exhibitionists and made a parade of their religion — 'made broad their phylacteries', to use the phrase in Matthew 23. There is a passage in the Talmud which divides the Pharisees into seven categories, in only one of which are they described as 'Pharisees of love'. Yet it was they who brought religion into the home and the daily life of the people, and it is no exaggeration to say that Judaism could not have survived without them when the national life of Israel and its religious centre at Jerusalem disappeared in A.D. 70.

There was also a small group of Apocalyptic Pharisees who believed that the world in its present state was soon to come to an end and looked to the advent of a Messiah to usher in a new order of peace and righteousness and love for all mankind. Josephus tells us that they were always urging people to follow them into the wilderness, and he mentions two 'false prophets', Theudas and a certain Egyptian, who were executed by the Roman governors when their promises to perform certain miracles proved a delusion. The religious sect of the Essenes (see below), who flourished in Palestine at the close of the Second Temple period, were close to these Pharisees in their religious outlook, though having their own specific beliefs and customs.

The Sadducees. In strong contrast to the Pharisees stood the Sadducees, the party of the 'establishment', both hierarchical and political, who identified themselves with the supposed descendants of Zadok the High Priest in the time of King David. They were the Hellenistic aristocracy, on friendly terms with Herod and the Roman governors. They upheld the Temple worship and its sacrificial system and accepted the written law of Moses but totally rejected the interpretative approach of the Oral Law. Thus the Pharisaical beliefs in the immortality of the soul, the existence of angels, and the coming of a Messianic era were in complete opposition to their whole ideology, which may be described as down to earth and existential. They had little or no permanent effect on the subsequent history of a people whose whole vision was characterized by 'immortal longings'.

The Essenes. More and more interest is being shown today in this sect, which arose in Palestine during the second century B.C. It consisted of a number of monastic groups which settled on the banks of the Jordan or in the hill country overlooking the Dead Sea. The etymology of the Greek name,

Essenes, by which they became known, is obscure. Some
think it may have come possibly from the Syriac *Hasya*,
'pious'. Until recently, our information about them came
only from Philo, the Alexandrian philosopher, and from
Josephus, who for a time lived among them, and, curiously
enough, the Roman naturalist, Pliny the Elder, who paid
them amazing tribute: 'a unique people, in the whole world
wonderful beyond all others; without women, giving up
sexual intercourse, without money, the companion of palm
trees. So, through a thousand generations, incredible to relate
the race is eternal, so fruitful to them is repentance in the life
of others' (Pliny 5.17). This has now been supplemented by
the scrolls of the Qumran community, which most scholars
agree was closely associated with the Essenes.

   Josephus tells us that they numbered about four thousand;
that they aimed to lead a life free from worldly contamination,
and practised extreme forms of asceticism. They adhered to
a strictly vegetarian diet, abstention from sexual intercourse
(except in some cases for the purpose of procreation), constant
ablution (every morning before their first meal they bathed
in fresh spring water), and communal ownership of all property. Their chief occupation was farming; they opposed
animal sacrifice and brought only offerings of flour and oil
to the Temple. From the Dead Sea Scrolls, we learn of the
strict rules of conduct collected in a 'Manual of Discipline'.
More interesting still, perhaps, was the belief of the group
that a 'Teacher of Righteousness', the founder of the movement, who had been put to death by a 'wicked priest', would
miraculously return to earth. Some scholars have, in fact,
gone so far as to identify this teacher with Jesus himself.

The Zealots. At the opposite end of the scale was a group who
believed that Jewish freedom and the future development of
their religion could only be secured by forceful resistance
against Roman domination. These were the Zealots or, in
Hebrew, the *Kannaim*, a generic name for all who show
themselves *zealous* for the honour of God or Israel. The
movement started when a Galilean named Judah urged his
fellow-countrymen to refuse to pay the taxes which the

Roman ethnarch, Quirinus, had imposed as the result of a census taken in A.D. 6. They fanatically opposed any action savouring of idolatry, such as bowing to the emperor's statue or even giving particulars for the census. They developed their own theological and messianic outlook, proclaiming God as the sole ruler of the Jewish people, fiercely combating mixed marriages on the part of Jews, and directing their struggle both against foreign rule and against those Jews who accepted it. Their violent methods earned for them the name of *Sicarii* (dagger-men) because they carried a *sica*, or dagger; Josephus has called them *lestai* (robbers). We have to remember, however, that Josephus was a supporter of Roman authority, and this may have impaired his judgement. The sentiment expressed by one of them bears, at any rate, the stamp of deep sincerity: 'Moreover, I believe that it is God who granted to us this favour, that we have it in our power to die nobly and in freedom.'

Jesus of Nazareth

It was in this complex religious scene that Jesus of Nazareth (or, to use his original name, Joshua ben Joseph) spent his boyhood. Though Christians are familiar with the events of his life and teaching through the writings of the New Testament and the teachings of the Church, it is important also to see him in relation to his Jewish background Thus, it is possible that he may have been one of the Apocalyptic Pharisees, whose sublime teaching and witness were based on the Torah, the Prophetic writings and contemporary rabbinic interpretations. Nevertheless, he brought a new emphasis and illumination, which were peculiarly his own, to bear on those traditional insights. These can be summed up in terms of his urgent and penetrating appeal to ordinary men and women to base their lives and actions on the dynamic of love — *agape*, to use the Greek word which best defines his concept, namely the love which entails suffering and sacrifice — as the one potent force capable of bringing them salvation. All this he summarized in the famous 'Sermon on the Mount', where his teaching is given practical shape and applied to human conduct of every kind. Most of it was already implicit in the

Prophetic messages as well as in the sayings of contemporary rabbis, for Jesus did not seek to abolish the Torah but to extend it. Yet the claim that he was the awaited Messiah, and the popular support he obtained, brought him into conflict with the Sadducaic priesthood which, as we have seen, was in close collusion with the Roman authorities. A political Sanhedrin decided to report him as a potential rebel to the then Procurator, Pontius Pilate, who sentenced him to be crucified — the Roman method of execution: this probably took place in A.D. 29 when he was about thirty years old.

It should be remembered, in any consideration of Jesus of Nazareth, that he was himself a faithful and practising Jew, born of a Jewish mother of the seed of David — Jewish scholars would also take the view that his father was a Jew — and that his friends and disciples were also Jews. It should also be remembered that it is in the crucifixion of Jesus that we find the roots of religious antisemitism, culminating in the charge of deicide — that bitter scourge of prejudice, intolerance, discrimination and persecution which has afflicted Jewry for centuries in every Christian country.

It is not possible in a book concerned with post-biblical Judaism to dwell at length upon the 'crucifixion story', but one of the most important steps taken to put right Christian teaching on this subject came in 1947, following the end of World War II. This was an emergency conference of Christians and Jews, called at Seelisberg in Switzerland to discuss the evils of antisemitism. Out of this conference, as a guide-line for Christian teachers, came a document called 'The Ten Points of Seelisberg', which is still of continuing formative value in the presentation of the New Testament narrative, the Seventh Point reading:

> Avoid presenting the Passion in such a way as to bring the odium of the killing of Jesus upon all Jews or upon Jews alone. It was only a section of the Jews in Jerusalem who demanded the death of Jesus, and the Christian message has always been that it was the sins of mankind which were exemplified by those Jews and the sins in which all men share that brought Christ to the Cross.

It was agreed by the compilers of the 'Ten Points' that

all Christian parents and teachers be made aware of the grave responsibility they assume in the presentation of the Passion Story, and of the risk they run, however unintentionally, of implanting an aversion in the conscious or sub-conscious minds of children by careless teaching. There is always a danger lest. . . the story of [the Saviour's] death be turned into an indiscriminate hatred of the Jews of all times, including those of our own day.

The crucifixion of Jesus of Nazareth was, of course, no isolated event, but had its counterpart in many Roman provinces where a cruel and repressive governor was responsible for administration. Execution was generally preceded by scourging, as in the case of Jesus, and there was a mocking of the victim by the coarse legionaries, together with other and worse indignities. To a thinking Jew, the death of Jesus means the death of yet one more Jewish martyr, whose only crime was that, in his whole-hearted zeal for the kingdom of God, he failed to pay lip-service to the kingdom of man. To the Christian, brought up largely on a distorted version of the event, it unfortunately gave the basis for centuries of oppression and annihilation.

Such statements as the 'Ten Points of Seelisberg', made immediately after the most fearful decimation of Jews in history, may seem mild enough in relation to the enormity of what was done, but signify the beginning of what we hope may become a total change in Christian attitudes.

Jews and the Christian Church
It was only after the death of Jesus that a small group of Palestinian Jews, led by his disciples, felt that they had received a new revelation through his birth, life and death. They formed themselves into the nucleus of the early Church, claiming that Jesus was the 'Son of God', born of a divine father and a virgin mother (the Incarnation), that he arose from the grave (the Resurrection) and that his early return to earth was to be expected (Advent or Second Coming). The Jerusalem Church still kept the traditional Judaism of

the Torah, but added to it the belief that, in accordance with Old Testament prophecy, the 'Son of Man' had appeared on earth, offering to man redemption and salvation through identification with their 'risen Lord'. The bulk of the Jews of that time, however, rejected these supernatural claims and, as we can read in the book of Acts, the ruling Sadducees went so far as to persecute the early Church as a heretical sect.

Paul of Tarsus

The whole position was aggravated and the parting of the ways between Church and Synagogue was finally brought about through the teachings of a unique personality, Paul of Tarsus. Paul was a Hellenized Jew, a tent-maker from the Roman province of Cilicia, now a small Turkish town in the centre of a cotton-growing district. When he came to live in Jerusalem, he was one of those who took part in persecuting the new movement, but, during a journey to Damascus, he had a vision which led him to accept the validity of the Christian sect and he then became one of its most active and formative witnesses. He especially regarded himself as an apostle of the new faith to the gentiles and, with great courage and often at the risk of his life, carried out his mission through a series of journeys to all the great centres of the Roman Empire.

It is no exaggeration to say that it was through the genius of Paul, as expressed in preaching and the writing of a number of letters, that Christianity took historical shape. He de-Judaized it to some extent by insisting that faith in Christ took precedence over adherence to the Torah. Moreover, with or without conscious effort on his part, he succeeded in making it acceptable to the Greco-Roman world by emphasizing its mystical aspect and bringing it closer to the contemporary mystery religions such as Mithraism. These mystery religions possessed one common factor in the belief that salvation could be won through identification with the life, death and resurrection of the particular Lord of the cult.

Jews in the Diaspora

It is sometimes assumed that Judaism has never been a proselytizing religion, but, though there have been periods of exclusiveness when a 'fence' was deliberately put 'round the Torah' and others when conversion carried with it the risk of capital punishment, this assumption is very far from actual fact. Especially during the Roman period, Judaism won adherents all over the Empire and, if we are to judge from a verse in Matthew's Gospel (23.15), the Pharisees were at pains to 'traverse sea and land to make a single proselyte'. Indeed, they seem to have had a considerable amount of success, since one of Nero's wives, Poppaea, became a convert, and the Senate actually passed legislation to prevent the spread of the religion.

It is true that many of the diaspora (that is, scattered, non-Palestinian) Jews later became converted to Christianity, but nevertheless traditional Jewish life continued in many parts of the Empire, and this was especially true of the community in Alexandria. These were largely Greek-speaking, and it was to satisfy their needs that the Hebrew Bible was translated into Greek in the form of the Septuagint, of which mention has already been made.

There was also a considerable Jewish community in Rome, as we can tell from such contemporary authors as Cicero, Horace and Juvenal. The latter indeed typified the general contempt felt for Judaism by pagan authors, when he referred to the Jewish code as 'all those dreary precepts Moses' mystic book contains'. Even the Stoic philosopher, Seneca, wrote of the Jews as a 'most villainous race' (*sceleratissima*) and attacked the observance of rest on the Sabbath as due to indolence: 'they waste a seventh part of life in leisure.'

Philo and Josephus

Much of the hostility towards Judaism found in Latin authors arose from the polemical writings of certain Greek writers at this period, notably the Alexandrian, Apion, whose works consisted of the crudest denigration of Jewish custom and belief. The roots of Alexandrian antisemitism lay probably in the rapid growth of Jewish population in the city, in their autonomous administration under the Ethnarchs, in the influence of their intellectual activities and, particularly, in the advance of the economic and civic power they wielded.

Apion's antisemitic writing produced its counterblast in the work of two outstanding Jewish writers, already mentioned, Philo and Josephus. The former, also an Alexandrian, attempted to meet the Greek challenge by interpreting the Hebrew Bible allegorically, so as to make its teachings consistent with Platonic philosophy. He had little effect on the main stream of subsequent Jewish thinking but exerted a vital influence on the Gnostic movement in Christianity — a movement with obscure origins, combining Greek philosophical ideas with a monotheistic basis, which was looked upon with disapproval by church and rabbis alike.

Josephus, the Jewish historian — who, as we have seen, later supported Rome and opposed Jewish resistance against the dominant power of the ancient world — refuted the attacks on Judaism in a disputation called *Contra Apionem*, in which he defended his religion against the monstrous travesties and misrepresentations so typical of contemporary and later polemical writing. He also wrote an account of the revolt of the Jews against Rome (A.D. 66-70) as well as a history of his people called *Antiquities of the Jews*. He was later taken prisoner and deported to Rome where he ended his days.

The Fall of Jerusalem and Bar Kokhba's Revolt

The rebellion against Rome, of which Josephus wrote, came as the result of the cruel oppression of one of the Governors of Judaea, Florus. At first successful, this revolt against Roman authority led to a long and bitter siege of Jerusalem by the Roman legionaries, first under the generalship of Vespasian (who returned to Rome to become Emperor in A.D. 69) and later under Titus. Finally, the city fell and the Temple was destroyed in A.D. 70. The triumphal Arch of Titus can still be seen in Rome depicting the carrying away of the Temple spoils.

This must have looked like the end of Judaism and the Jewish people, but in reality it proved to be a new beginning. For the basic message of the Torah and the Prophets was universal in character and independent of both geography and political institutions. Centres of Jewish life and learning with their synagogues and rabbinic schools arose all over the Diaspora. It is significant that, during the siege of Jerusalem, a great rabbi, Johanan ben Zakkai, obtained leave from Vespasian to transfer his activities to nearby Jabneh which became the seat of an important rabbinic academy and of a reconstructed Sanhedrin. Here, round about the year A.D. 90, an event of great biblical importance took place under the famous rabbi, Akivah ben Joseph. Already, most of the books which today comprise the Hebrew Bible (known to Christians as the Old Testament) had come to be accepted as having a special degree of authority and sanctity. Of the three sections into which the Hebrew Bible is divided, two, the Law (or the Torah) and the Prophets (which included the books of Samuel and Kings), were recognized as canonical works, or as belonging to the Canon of Holy Scripture. The word 'canon' is of Semitic origin but acquired a Greek form: it means a measuring-rod — hence, measure or standard. About the third section, however, there were still uncertainties. Known as 'the Writings', it contained such books as Psalms, Proverbs and Job. Doubts about such books as Ecclesiastes and the Song of Songs still remained, however, and it was not until about A.D. 90 that these doubts were resolved and the definitive decision taken to include them and to close for all time the 'canon' of the Hebrew Bible.

Early in the following century, there was an attempt to restore Jewish nationhood as the result of the Emperor Hadrian's proposal to turn Jerusalem into a pagan city and rebuild the Temple as a shrine sacred to Jupiter Capitolinus. When he came up against the fanatical faith of the Jewish people in the one supreme God, he determined — following the example of Antiochus Epiphanes — to put an end to Judaism by producing a series of decrees forbidding the observance of the Sabbath, the rite of circumcision and the study of the Torah. This led to a widespread and for a time successful revolt carried out with messianic fervour under Bar Kokhba, a revolutionary leader who attempted to restore the national existence of the Jewish people. His name meant 'Son of a Star', and Rabbi Akiva acclaimed him with the words: 'A star hath stepped forth out of Jacob.' Finally, however, the revolt was crushed by the Roman legions, and Judaism became a proscribed religion throughout the Empire.

Christianity and the Roman Empire
In spite of initial persecution, particularly under the rule of Nero and Diocletian, Christianity gradually spread through the Roman Empire. From small beginnings on the part of scattered communities (about which we can read in Pliny the Younger's *Letters to Trajan*), showing the greatest courage and devotion to their faith, it achieved a dominant role in Roman life. Eventually, when the Emperor Constantine was converted, it actually became the official state religion. This had its effect upon the Jewish people, and their persecution, as an unbelieving minority, soon followed. The Day of Rest was transferred from Saturday to Sunday, and the Jewish rite of circumcision was again forbidden. There was some respite under Julian the Apostate (A.D. 361-3) when all religions were tolerated, but this was short-lived. During the declining years of the Empire, and especially under Justinian, the synagogues continued to suffer persecution and the Jewish communities lost their last vestiges of liberty.

4

THE TALMUDIC PERIOD

The School at Jabneh
It has been said that the Romans were the most tolerant of
ancient peoples. When, however, Vespasian allowed Rabbi
Johanan to escape from Jerusalem during the siege (there is
a legend that he was borne in a coffin by his disciples) and to
establish a rabbinic school in Jabneh, it is doubtful if he
realized the full significance of his action in relation to the
subsequent story of the Jewish people. Probably he attached
little or no importance to the rabbi's petition. But actually
the foundation of the school at Jabneh was a turning-point in
Jewish history.

The destruction of the Temple and the capture of Jerusalem
had put an end to all the outward and visible forms of Jewish
corporate existence, such as the priesthood and the secular
religious Councils (Sanhedrin). This new rabbinic school
succeeded in salvaging from what appeared to be a total
wreck those values of piety and learning which were basic to
the whole concept of Torah. As one historian has put it, 'the
day of the priest was over. The day of the rabbi had come.'

Gradually the academy at Jabneh became the supreme
religious authority for the Jewish Diaspora. A new Sanhedrin
was created whose judicial procedure is described in one of
the rabbinic compilations called the Mishnah (see further in
this chapter):

> The court sat in a semicircle, so that the members might
> be able to see one another. Two clerks of the court stood
> in front of them, one on the right and one on the left, to
> record the votes of the judges who acquitted and of those
> who condemned. Three rows of scholars sat in front of
> them, each having his own special place. When it was
> necessary to fill a vacancy among the judges, one of those
> in the first row was chosen. Immediately one in the second
> row took a seat in the first, and one from the third in the

second row. A member of the general gathering was then chosen to fill the vacancy in the third row. He did not step directly into the seat of the last person, but took the last seat in the third row.

But more important than questions of organization was the adaptation which exponents of Judaism had to make to ensure that its ethics and outlook applied to new conditions. This must have been something like a revolution in thought. Old loyalties to nation and shrine had gone for ever. Something different, therefore, had to take their place if Judaism was to mean anything in a new situation. This is just what the Rabbis provided.

Two illustrations can be selected from the contemporary writings to show what this something different was. One comes from Johanan's own teaching on the need for social righteousness. The story goes that, one day when he and his pupil Rabbi Joshua were passing by the ruins of the Holy City, the latter sighed:

'Woe is us that our Temple is desolate!'

'My son,' said Rabbi Johanan, 'be not grieved. We have something of equal value in its place — the practice of charity and loving-kindness.'

The other shows the new religious approach of a younger rabbi, Joshua ben Hananyah, who accompanied Johanan when he moved to Jabneh during the siege of Jerusalem. Hananyah has been called 'the last Pharisee' by a modern writer (Joseph Podro) and he opposed both the nationalist movement of the Zealots — who looked to a restoration of the political state — as well as the religious fundamentalism of the school of Shammai: 'This is no longer the time to increase the Oral Law; we must winnow the grain already accumulated.' During all this stormy period his one object was to revive the broken heart of Israel and give his people a new sense of unity and purpose based on the Hillelite doctrine (see p. 13) of humility and love of mankind.

Spread of the Schools
As a result of Hadrian's policy of suppression following on

the Bar Kokhba revolt, the college at Jabneh lost its central position in Jewish learning and eventually had to be closed. Fortunately, similar houses of learning had been founded in many of the scattered Jewish settlements, and the practice and study of Judaism were kept alive.

This defiance of the imperial edict was due to the very special kind of resourcefulness and courage which characterized the whole rabbinic ethos at this time. It can be illustrated from a story about Rabbi Akiva to be found in the Talmud (see p. 45).

A man named Pappus once found Rabbi Akiva expounding the Torah in public, in defiance of Hadrian's edict.

'Are you not afraid of the Romans, Akiva?' asked Pappus in amazement.

'I will tell you a story,' replied the Rabbi. 'A fox was walking along a river bank when he saw a shoal of fish scurrying in all directions.

"Why are you fleeing?" asked the fox.

"Because of the fishermens' nets," they answered.

"Come on dry land and be safe with me", suggested the fox.

"Are you the wisest of beasts?" exclaimed the fish, "If in our own element we live in fear, how much more should we dread the dry land, which means inevitable death to us!"

'So', went on Akiva, 'it may be true that we endanger our lives by studying the Torah. But it is our element and the source of our life. We shall assuredly find ourselves in worse danger if we neglect it.'

After the fall of Jabneh, the rabbinic scholars moved especially to the towns in Galilee so that they might be further away from Roman military domination. At one of them, Usha, the Sanhedrin was set up afresh, but the centre soon shifted from there to other towns such as Sepphoris and Tiberias. Soon, however, it was found necessary to move to even more distant parts, and the great academies of Babylon became the real centres of Jewish culture and learning. It was they, *par excellence*, that provided the basis, both scholarly and practical, for Jewish life in all its subsequent developments.

Judah the Prince

After the death of Hadrian, his edict making the practice of Judaism virtually illegal was repealed by the Emperor Antoninus Pius (c. A.D. 136). He, like his more famous successor Marcus Aurelius, brought the principles of the great philosophy of Stoicism, stemming from ancient Athens, to bear on government and the imperial administration. Jewish learning gained a new lease of life, and a beginning was made to provide elementary education for Jewish boys and girls from the age of six or seven. By the fourth century this became universal, at least for boys, for the first time in history, and this was due to the immense importance the rabbis have always laid on the training of the young. One early rabbinic passage runs, 'The world is sustained by the breath of school-children' and, in the Talmud, there was even a discussion about the ideal size for a class — the rabbinic decision being that this should be twenty-five!

At this time the old religious court called the Sanhedrin ceased to function and authority passed to the successors of Johanan ben Zakkai who came to be referred to as the Patriarchate. This reached its fullest development and recognition by scattered Jewry under the leadership of Judah, (c. A.D. 135-220) whose father and grandfather (both named Gamaliel) had both been Patriarchs. This remarkable man was not only an outstanding scholar but something of a royal figure who, it is said, became the friend of the Emperor Marcus Aurelius himself. He possessed such authority over the people that he became known to subsequent generations as Judah ha-Nasi (the Prince). He revived the Hebrew language (which had been displaced for colloquial purposes by Aramaic) for his household, considering it to be, together with Greek, the only civilized language for human intercourse. Later in his life he retired, owing to ill-health, to Sepphoris and it is here that he compiled the great authoritative code known as the Mishnah, which became the standard embodiment of the Oral Law and the basis for all subsequent Judaism.

The Mishnah

It is often said of English law that it has never been codified but is an accumulated jurisprudence resting on an infinite succession of court decisions. This, to a large extent, applies to the ancient Mishnah (c. A.D. 200) which really means 'teaching' or repetition — Mishnah Torah, repetition or re-counting of Torah. What had happened was that the original Jewish code, the written Torah, consisting of the first five books of the Bible, had ceased to apply in many of its details to the contemporary life of widely scattered communities, and needed to be reinterpreted to meet the needs of a much-changed form of society. This was precisely the problem with which the rabbis had to deal between the periods of Hillel and Judah the Prince. These authorities on the Oral Law were called the *Tannaim* (meaning those who repeat, and who teach their disciples to repeat, with the object of memorizing) and it was their opinions or *'responsa'* which were now collected and published in the Mishnah.

In this way, one of the most complex and erudite, almost encyclopaedic types of literature came to be published. It consisted of six strands or Orders, each subdivided into a number of Tractates. The subjects they treated came under the following headings: (1) Seeds (i.e. land), (2) Festivals, (3) Women (i.e. marriage), (4) Civil Law, (5) the Temple Service and (6) Purity. Here was the oldest collection, apart from the Pentateuch (or Torah), of Jewish legislative writings. It comprised and supplemented the Torah, so that together they became the fulfilment of divine teaching or revelation to the Jewish people throughout their history.

The Gemara

Typically the compilation of the Mishnah brought no finality to Jewish thought and insight. For the next three hundred years (A.D. 201-500) a new type of rabbinic teacher came to dominate the scene and take the place of the Tannaim. These were called Amoraim, or expounders, and they set them-selves the task of interpreting, through elaborate processes of analysis and thought, the findings of the Mishnah. At this time (see p. 54) the centres of learning shifted from Palestine to Babylon where two outstanding schools were founded at Sura and Pumbeditha — compared by one historian with Oxford and Cambridge.

The Babylonian Jews, in fact, began to enjoy something like autonomy under their rulers, who made full use of their initiative and intelligence in keeping the imperial power of Rome at bay. Not only were they able to retain their synagogues, schools for children and houses of learning but, through their elected leader, called the Exilarch (or *Resh Galuta*), they obtained a kind of political recognition in the eyes of the government. It is true that the overthrow of the Empire by Persia led to further Jewish oppression, but their position was infinitely happier than that occupied by their brothers who lived under the Roman *imperium*.

It was in Babylon, therefore, that the second great rabbinic work, called the Gemara, was compiled a little before A.D. 500. It owed its inspiration especially to two brilliant legal minds, those of Abba the Tall, later called Rav, *the* rabbi *par excellence*, and a certain Samuel who was not only an expert in jurisprudence but also a physician and astronomer. A second but less important Gemara was compiled in Palestine, but it is the Babylonian compilation which came to exercise the paramount influence and authority in subsequent Jewish history. The Mishnah and Gemara together were called the Talmud (learning), and the whole of this important, formative period as well as the religious and literary development which flowed from it were henceforth referred to by the term Talmudic.

Halakhah and Haggadah

The Talmud was the outstanding literary product of post-biblical Judaism, and something further must be said of the peculiar qualities of this unique compendium and of the particular brand of genius it portrays. For we have, here, a miscellaneous compilation that ranged over a vast number of areas, jurisprudence, philosophy, history, legend and homily. In fact, it may be said to represent the experience of a widely scattered people during 500 years of its existence.

Two identifiable strands run through the whole of this literature, called respectively by Jewish scholars Halakhah and Haggadah. The word Halakhah is derived from a Hebrew root meaning 'to walk' and the term was used to describe the legalistic, practical 'way of life' teachings to be found scattered throughout the Talmud. The other section, called Haggadah, contained the less precise, more imaginative thoughts of the sages: 'the Humanities of Rabbinic teaching' as they have been called. Here history, folk-lore, biography are inextricably interwoven with ethics, hygiene, astronomy and logic.

Inevitably the Halakhic element came to be expressed in dialectic and it can best be appreciated by selecting a typical passage. The Mishnah contains a Sabbath regulation that 'one shall not read by the lamplight' — presumably because one might be tempted to snuff the wick if the flame burnt low. In the Gemara, this regulation is discussed at great length. Here is a quotation, with many explanatory insertions, for the Talmud is almost unreadably concise:

> Rabbah (a Babylonian scholar) said (that one should not read by the lamp) even if it be placed (far out of reach, say,) the height from the ground of two men, or two storeys, or even on top of ten houses, one above the other. (That is) 'one may not read'. But it does not say two may not read together (for then one can guard the other against snuffing the wick). Against this supposition, however, there is a tradition that 'neither one nor two together' (may read). Said Rabbi Elazar: 'There is no contradiction here. The Mishnah allows (two people to read together) so long as they read the same subject. But the tradition (forbids it only if) they are reading *different* subjects.'

And in that manner the subject is continued.

And here are a few samples of Haggadah, the more imaginative form of teaching:

> All Israelites are mutually accountable for each other. In a boat at sea one of them began to bore a hole in the bottom of the boat. On being remonstrated with, he answered: 'I am only boring under my own seat.' 'Yes,' said his comrades, 'but when the sea rushes in we shall all be drowned with you.' So it is with Israel. Its weal or its woe is in

the hands of every individual Israelite.

Another example of this deeply humanistic insight of the rabbinic mind as expressed in the pattern of the Haggadah is the following:

Rabbi Meir sat during the whole of the Sabbath-day in the School instructing the people. During his absence from the house his two sons died, both of them of uncommon beauty and enlightened in the Law. His wife bore them to her bed-chamber, and spread a white covering over their bodies. In the evening Rabbi Meir came home. 'Where are my sons?' he asked. 'I repeatedly looked round the School and I did not see them there.' She gave him a cup of wine. He praised the Lord at the going out of the Sabbath, drank and again asked, 'Where are my sons?' 'They will not be afar off,' she said, and placed food before him that he might eat. When he had said grace after the meal, she thus addressed him: 'With thy permission, I would ask thee one question.' 'Ask it then,' he replied. 'A few days ago a person entrusted some jewels into my custody, and now he demands them of me; should I give them back again?' 'This is a question,' said the Rabbi, 'which my wife should not have thought it necessary to ask. What! wouldst thou hesitate to restore to every one his own?' 'No,' she replied; 'but yet I thought it best not to restore them without acquainting you therewith.' She then led him to the chamber, and took the white covering from the dead bodies. 'Ah, my sons! my sons!' loudly lamented the father. 'My sons! the light of my eyes!' The mother turned away and wept bitterly. At length she took her husband by the hand, and said: 'Didst thou not teach me that we must not be reluctant to restore that which was entrusted to our keeping? See — the Lord gave, and the Lord hath taken away; blessed be the name of the Lord!'

The Meaning of Midrash

The humanism of the rabbis found perhaps its completest expression in what is called Midrash (from a verb meaning 'to seek' or 'inquire'), a type of literature which originated in Palestine during the Talmudic period. Midrash means in particular the search for new meaning, other than literal, in the Scriptures. It is biblical commentary designed to extract the fullest implication from each passage. It also expounds the non-legal portions of the Scriptures. Like parts of the Gemara, it was homiletic in character, and some of its stories, sayings and legends contain a message which goes to the heart of many of the social, racial and international problems which beset mankind today. For example: 'I call heaven and earth to witness that whether it be Jew or heathen, man or woman, free or bondman — only according to their acts does the Divine spirit rest upon them.' Again, a story is told of Abraham who was asked for a night's lodging by a fire-worshipper. When he refused to pray to the true God, Abraham, in righteous indignation, drove him from his tent. But that night Abraham had a vision in which the Almighty appeared to him and said, 'Abraham, I have borne with that foolish old man for seventy years. Could you not bear with him for one night?'

Some of the pithiest Midrashic sayings are to be found in a compilation called *Pirke Avot*, the 'Ethics of the Fathers' (from one of the Tractates of the Mishnah itself). This was incorporated, like much else of this early literature, in the Jewish Prayer Book still used in modern synagogues. Typical of these 'jewels, five fingers wide' is Hillel's 'Let thy house be open wide: let the poor be the members of it.' There follows a warning against 'much gossip' (particularly with women!), and 'judge not thy neighbour until thou art come into his place'. But perhaps the most pertinent one of all is the one that deals, lightly but profoundly, with the whole basis of self-confidence: 'If I am not for myself, who will be for me? And being for myself alone, what am I? And if not now, when?'

Influence of the Talmud on Subsequent Judaism

Judaism today and throughout the ages is based on both the Written and Oral Law, and here it must be stressed that the Talmud has had an influence on its development almost equal with that of the Old Testament itself. Not only did this vast literature influence its religion in a ritualistic sense, but the whole of Jewish life came to be regulated by its rulings. Here, it must be remembered that in Jewish thought there is no ultimate dichotomy between what is called the spiritual and material, since both derive from the same universal source. Thus it is to the Talmud one must go if one wants to know about Jewish attitudes and practices with regard to such matters as contract, marriage, divorce, property, relations with non-Jews, obligation to the secular state and so on.

The Talmud was, however, reviled and held up to scorn and derision by those who sought to destroy Judaism and convert its followers to Christianity during the Middle Ages. Nor has it lacked critics amongst sections of the Jewish people themselves, who came to regard many of its enactments as out of date and isolationist, particularly during the period of emancipation. But this must not lead us into the error of underestimating its significance in both the creation and preservation of Jewish identity throughout history or detracting from its intrinsic worth and merit as one of the great religious textbooks of all time.

This has been eloquently stated by a modern Anglican scholar, the Revd Dr James Parkes, in his book *Prelude to Dialogue*, p.101:

> Jewry survived not because of the nobility of the prophets, a nobility which all men can perceive for themselves, but because of the Talmud, that strange, incomprehensible, and (I believe) unique amalgam of laws, pithy sayings, tedious lecture notes, half-finished reports of discussions, and what not, which formed the moral, recreational, and intellectual pabulum of Jews for a millennium.

> We can see that the rabbis left the mind free where the other monotheisms bound it by the line between orthodoxy and heresy: we can see that they preserved the separation of the Jews without enforcing their isolation; we can see, in fact, that somehow their Talmud gave those services which Toynbee believes the Jewish diaspora could give to the increasingly rootless non-Jewish world. But the

diaspora was preserved by the Talmud because within its voluminous and confused pages was a root, a unity, an identity, which made it a 'portable homeland'. There was no central authority, there was no hierarchy of control, but Jews were identifiable as Jews from China to the Atlantic. For their Jewishness has a common root.

The Final Code

In spite of its remarkable qualities, the Talmud is an untidy, complex amalgam of laws, stories, history and *obiter dicta*, so that if, in later times, a precise answer was required to any legal or moral problem, it could not be found without a great deal of research. It followed that in course of time it became necessary to draw up some more precise codification, and this received its final form in what is called the *Shulhan Arukh* ('ordered table'). Its compiler was a Spanish rabbi, Joseph Caro, the last great codifier of rabbinic law and the greatest Talmudic authority of the sixteenth century. He was born in 1480 and was brought by his father to Turkey as a result of the Spanish Expulsion. In 1536 Caro settled in Safed in Galilee, where he founded a Talmudic school from which many famous scholars graduated. He was both scholar and mystic, and carried out his task of codifying the Talmud with such thoroughness and efficiency that his work became an authoritative textbook for the interpretation of Jewish law and practice for orthodox Jewish communities throughout the world. There was some danger, here, of fossilization which for a considerable period prevented the kind of free development which had characterized the earlier history of Judaism, but in the Middle Ages it certainly preserved the Talmudic spirit and discipline which kept the scattered Jewish communities from disintegration and gave them a unity and purpose. Even today, when there are a number of dissident sects within the Jewish people, there is a common, perhaps rather flippant, saying among Jews which pays a tacit tribute to Joseph Caro: 'every Jew has his own *Shulhan Arukh!*'

5

JEWISH LIFE UNDER ISLAM

Mohammed

A highly controversial figure now dominates the world scene, that of an Arab camel-driver called Mohammed who was born in the city of Mecca about the year A.D. 570. He was a man of deep religious insight and fervour, who felt a divine call to proclaim a new faith to his kinsfolk, the Arab people. Hitherto they had worshipped some three hundred gods, the chief of whom was believed to have his shrine in Mecca — a mysterious black stone — to which pilgrims used to flock from all parts of Arabia.

This new religion, Islam, which Mohammed taught, was strictly monotheistic and based to a large extent on the Bible. It revered the great biblical figures such as Moses, Abraham and Jesus, the latter being considered the first adherent of the Islamic faith. The holy book of Islam, the *Koran*, contains the utterances of Mohammed during his prophetic career, and reveals the great influence exercised by Judaism — spread to some extent by Jewish settlers in Arab lands, fleeing from Roman persecution. The *Koran* reproduces many Jewish as well as Christian ideas, mentioning several precepts of Jewish law, and even containing Hebrew loan-words. Biblical tales and allusions to events in ancient Hebrew history are frequent.

Perhaps the surest way to understand the deep experiences of the Islamic religion is through a study of prayer — for instance, the prayer of pilgrims to Mecca:

O God, I ask of thee a perfect faith, a sincere assurance, a reverent heart, a remembering tongue, a good conduct of commendation and a true repentance, repentance before death, rest at death and forgiveness and mercy after death, clemency at the reckoning, victory in paradise and escape from the fire, by Thy mercy, O mighty One, O Forgiver. Lord, increase me in knowledge and join me unto the good.

Again:

> Thou art my Lord, I thy servant.
> I have wronged myself and I confess my sin.
> Forgive me then all my sins, for there is none that
>   forgiveth sins save Thee.

In spite, however, of the loftiness of much of its teaching and liturgy, Islam made certain concessions to the materialistic outlook of its devotees and was ruthless in its manner of propagation.

The religion spread so rapidly in Mohammed's home town, Mecca, that the leading citizens began to be afraid lest the new monotheism should destroy the significance and centrality of the local shrine. They, therefore, plotted to put its leader to death and this led to the famous flight of Mohammed to the rival town of Medina, known in subsequent history as the *Hegira* ('Emigration' or 'Exodus'). This flight, which took place in A.D. 622, is regarded by Moslems right up to the present day as the most formative event of their history, and from it they still date their calendar.

Mohammed's Attitude to Judaism and the Jews

The main emphases in the new religion were prayer, cleanliness, fasting and almsgiving. All these were also an integral part of the practice of Judaism, and it might therefore be thought that Mohammed would welcome as allies the Jews who lived in Medina and elsewhere among the Arab communities. He did, in fact, look to them for support. But the central creed of Islam was that 'there is but one God, Allah, and Mohammed is his prophet', and enough has been said about Judaism and its relation to the Torah for it to be realized that it was this corollary that could never be acceptable. *Mutatis mutandis*, the same could be said of Christianity. The *Koran*, which constantly emphasizes the importance of worldly values and possessions and in general caters for man's earthly desires, could never, in Jewish eyes, take the place of the Torah.

Mohammed, finding that he could not win the favour of the Jewish communities and provoked, perhaps, by some lampoons which ridiculed him, written by the Jews of Medina,

turned bitterly against them. He offered them alternatives
of conversion or death and, when they refused the former,
his followers forcibly attacked them. In spite of some heroic
resistance, they were finally driven out of their north Arabian
settlements. At the same time, Jewish features which had
been retained in the new religion were transformed. Worshippers in future had to turn their faces towards Mecca instead
of Jerusalem: a whole month of fasting, *Ramadan*, took the
place of the Day of Atonement, and Friday became the holy
day instead of Saturday, the Jewish Sabbath.

Position of the Jews under the Caliphate

The story of the Arab (and Islamic) conquest of half the
known world that followed Mohammed's death in 632 is
too long to be told here. Suffice it to say that within twenty-
five years complete mastery had been established over Egypt,
Palestine, Syria, Babylonia and Persia, and it took only another
twenty-five for Islam to gain supremacy along all the Northern
coast of Africa and in most of the Spanish peninsula. Only
the power of Charlemagne and the newly established Holy
Roman Empire prevented Islam from crossing the Pyrenees
and perhaps dominating the whole of Europe.

The newly won territory, which stretched from the Atlantic
to the Ganges, was divided into five main provinces (ruled
over by successors of Mohammed who were called Caliphs)
namely, Persia, Syria, Egypt, Africa and Spain. Jerusalem
was captured from the Romans in 638 and the Caliph Omar
cleared the ground on which the Temple had stood, erecting
a Mosque which stands there to this day.

A more tolerant attitude to non-Moslems, both Jews and
Christians, prevailed when, less than a century later, the
Caliphate was centred in Baghdad. This meant that the various
Jewish communities in the Moslem countries no longer
suffered from violence or persecution. They were, however,
still subjected to various disabilities. They had to wear
special dress, were subjected to a poll-tax and were forbidden
to build new synagogues or occupy any position of authority
over the faithful. In practice, however, many of these restrictions were ignored and some Jews did rise to positions of

eminence under the Caliphate. In particular, they became a kind of bridge between the Moslem East and the Christian West when the barriers of language made trading and commerce exceedingly difficult. Jews living on both sides of the 'curtain' had a common language of their own, namely Hebrew, and at the same time were able to pick up the languages of those among whom they lived. Hence arose their role of world traders as well as of bankers and experts in finance, which had an important effect on their subsequent history.

The Gaonim

Under the Caliphate, the centre of Jewish life and teaching was still in Babylonia and the position of the *Resh Galuta* or Exilarch as the official representative of Jewry grew tremendously in prestige. He was regarded as both the spiritual and temporal ruler of Jewry and actually became a member of the Baghdad court. The office was hereditary, and it was popularly supposed that its holders were the descendants of David. Not only was the installation carried out with all the pomp and ceremony associated with coronations, but it was said that every fifth day the Exilarch paid a visit to the Caliph's court accompanied by an escort of Jewish and Moslem riders and was placed on a throne opposite that of the Caliph himself.

Next in importance in the temporal sphere, but more important in the religious, were the heads of the two academies already mentioned at Sura and Pumbeditha. They came to be called Gaonim (plural of *Gaon*, meaning Excellency) and their fame was such throughout Jewry that this whole period (roughly from the sixth to the thirteenth and even fourteenth century) is known as the Gaonate. It was the function of the Gaonim to spread knowledge of the Talmud throughout the scattered Jewish communities, and their *responsa* (literature presenting written decisions and rulings given by rabbis on questions addressed to them by individuals and communities seeking guidance) came to be invested with an authority which affected not only political and religious decisions at a high level but also the activities of everyday life. When, for instance, about 883, an impostor calling himself Eldad the Danite appeared in North Africa, claiming to belong to the Lost Ten Tribes and to have special knowledge of their ways and customs, it was to Gaon Zama that the local sages appealed for guidance.

The most famous of these Gaonim were Sherira, the historian, Hai, an independent thinker acquainted with Plato and Aristotle and, above all, Saadyah ben Joseph. As time went on, a certain tension grew up between the Exilarch and the Gaonim, between, that is to say, the civil and religious authorities, of a kind which has bedevilled human relationships in the history of so many peoples. In the Jewish scene it had at this period consequences so serious that it virtually put an end to both types of authority.

Karaite Movement

As so often happens in a situation of this kind, the tension suddenly broke into open schism as the result of an event which, at first, seemed almost irrelevant to the issues involved. About A.D. 760 a dispute arose with regard to the succession to the post of Exilarch, when the heads of the academies refused to appoint the Exilarch's eldest son, Anan ben David, as his successor, but preferred his younger brother. Anan refused to yield and proclaimed himself Exilarch. Imprisoned as a rebel (767), he pleaded that he and his supporters held a religion different from that of other Jews and, on his release, he became the leader of a separate Jewish sect, the Karaites, whose main feature was opposition to the Talmudic traditions. Anan threw over the whole rabbinic interpretation which had accumulated in the Talmud and reverted to the Bible as the sole basis of Judaism and the only valid religious authority.

The unity of Judaism and the Jewish people was shattered and for the next 200 years there was bitter controversy between Anan's party called the Karaites (from *Karah*, to read) and the Rabbanites who stuck to the tradition of the Oral Law.

The Karaites could, perhaps, be described as among the first fundamentalists in religious history. The movement bears some resemblance to that of the Sadducees and was perhaps

equally rigid, pedantic and uninspired. The dietary laws, for
instance, were extended to cover an even greater number of
animals as prohibited for food, and numerous fasts were
instituted. The Sabbath became a day of gloom, as no light
or fire was allowed in Jewish homes, and there was a prohibi-
tion on leaving the home during the Sabbath. In the case of
illness no doctors were to be consulted since, according to
scripture, 'the Lord is thy healer'. Anything in the nature of
mystical interpretation (Kabbalah, see p. 94) was regarded
as completely heretical. (See Rabbi Selvin Goldberg's book,
Karaite Liturgy, p. 27)

Nevertheless, the movement spread far and wide and
became a serious threat to the whole rabbinic outlook, mainly
because of its appeal to strict believers. Some Karaite ideas
were borrowed from current Arabic philosophy, and the movement is said even to have received support from a number of
Christians. But as time went on its leaders, notably Benjamin
of Nehawend, found that they had to have recourse to exactly
the same kind of modifications as rabbinism and they
succeeded in presenting a form of Judaism which could
appeal to an increasing number of followers.

Rabbi Saadyah
In spite of this, the whole Karaite movement received its
death sentence through the opposition of one of the most
learned and enlightened rabbis of all times, Saadyah ben
Joseph. He was born in Egypt of humble parents in 882 and
came into prominence as a result of controversy with a
Palestinian rabbi, called Ben Meir, who attempted, in the
year 921, to alter the Jewish calendar, proclaiming that the
Passover festival should be celebrated two days earlier than
the officially accepted date. This was really an effort to dis-
credit the supremacy of the Babylonian schools, which had
long been the repository of traditional Judaism, and Saadyah,
whose knowledge of Halakhic custom was unrivalled, immediately rose to champion the official rabbinic calendar.
A year later, Rabbi Meir received a crushing defeat, and the
Babylonian authorities were reinstated in world Jewish opinion
through the learning and energy of this young Egyptian scholar.

In 928 the office of Gaon of Sura became vacant and, in spite of the fact that he did not belong to the official rabbinic entourage, the then Exilarch, David ben Zakkai, appointed Saadyah to the post. He proved an incorruptible judge, and this eventually led him into conflict with his patron on a question of signing a legal document in which the latter had some private interest. The dispute lasted for seven years and Saadyah was forced to retire from office, but, being a man of considerable magnanimity, he bore no grudge, and a reconciliation took place on the festival of Purim in the year 937. The struggle, however, had taken its toll of him and, after a period of bad health, he died in 942 at the age of fifty.

Decline of Karaism

It has been said that the career of Saadyah saved authentic rabbinic Judaism from its greatest enemy — 'threatening the existence of tradition more even than the fall of Jerusalem'. He gave new life to rabbinism, broadened its outlook, and furnished it with a philosophic basis which has ensured its vitality and development right up to the present day.

The method he used was to meet his opponents on their own ground, but with a more penetrating insight and scholarship than any of them possessed. The Karaites, as explained before, reverted to biblical authority, so Saadyah translated the Bible into Arabic, the spoken language of the vast majority of Jews living in the Moslem world. He was thus able to demonstrate to ordinary people how untenable was the Karaite fundamentalism and how essential the Oral tradition in preserving a living form of Judaism. His other literary works were a Hebrew grammar in Arabic, an edition of the Prayer Book and a philosophical work called *Beliefs and Opinions*, through which Greek metaphysical thought, in Arab dress, permeated the Jewish world and produced a philosophic basis for traditional Judaism. All this had an effect on the later development of Karaism itself, where exponents began to show less rigidity and greater human insight. The movement survived as a small sect, and a few of its adherents are still to be found in Turkey and parts of southern Persia.

Spanish Caliphate

After the death of Saadyah, the influence of the Gaonim gradually declined, though two outstanding figures of the Gaonic
period were still to come. One was Rabbi Sherira (Gaon from
968 to 998) and the other his son, Rabbi Hai. The former was
consulted by the new school at Kairwan in North Africa, which
formed a bridge between Eastern and Western Jewish communities, on six questions relating to the authority of the
Talmud. This led to a lengthy and important historical Epistle,
written by Sherira in 992 in response to the inquiry.

Such was the regard in which father and son were held that,
on the Sabbath following Sherira's death, the passage read
was the one from the Book of Numbers in which Moses asks
God 'to set apart' a man:

Moses said to the Lord, 'Let the Lord, the God of the
spirits of all flesh, appoint a man over the congregation,
who shall go out before them and come in before them,
who shall lead them out and bring them in; that the congregation of the Lord may not be as sheep which have
no shepherd. (Num. 27.15-17)

This was followed by the chapter in 1 Kings 2.12 dealing
with the last days of David, and when the line was reached,
'so Solomon sat upon the throne of David his father', these
words were added: 'And Hai sat upon the throne of Sherira
his father.'

Hai (998-1038) was the last of the great Gaonim whose
responsa commanded universal respect. From this time onwards, the centre of Jewish religious interest gradually shifted
from Babylon and the East to Spain. This was largely due to
certain internal convulsions in the Moslem world, during
which the Baghdad Caliphate, which had given official
recognition to the Jews and to the Exilarch as their representative, collapsed and was succeeded by a number of minor
caliphates. These started to oppress all non-believers, both
Jewish and Christian, causing a great migration of the Eastern
Jewish communities to the Spanish Caliphate where they
obtained security and were often held in considerable respect.
Thus, for the next 400 years, the most important developments
in Jewish life and learning were to be found in Moslem Spain.

Hasdai and the Khazars

The tolerant rule of the Spanish Caliphate enabled Jews to enter every walk of the national and social life. They became peasants, farmers, craftsmen and physicians. The more gifted of them rose to positions of great influence in the diplomatic sphere. The first of these Jewish celebrities in the Spanish scene was Hasdai Ibn Shaprut (c. A.D. 915-970) who owed his political prestige to the fact that he was both a physician and a Latin scholar. Latin was the international language of the Christian Church for both letters and diplomacy, and Hasdai became the Caliph's adviser and was employed with brilliant success on foreign missions. Thus, when Otto I, the Holy Roman Emperor, sent an embassy to Cordova, it was Hasdai who was deputed to treat with it. Later he was sent to Sancho III, the King of Leon (a Christian state), both as diplomatic envoy and — here his medical knowledge came in — to cure him of his excessive corpulence. His dual expertise was again put to use when he translated Dioscorides' work on botany from its Latin form into Arabic, so that it became available to the Moslem medical schools in Spain and eventually to the whole of mediaeval Europe.

Preoccupation with politics and science did not, however, weaken Hasdai's central enthusiasm for Judaism and the Jewish people. He became a great patron of learning and laid the foundations of Spanish-Jewish scholarship which had a profound influence on all subsequent Jewish thought and literature. Of special interest was his correspondence with the Khazars. These were a semi-barbaric people living in what today is called the Russian Ukraine, who, early in the eighth century, became converted to Judaism. In those days, people's religion, like their politics, was very much what their rulers decided, and when a certain Bulan, the ruling prince of the Khazars, formally adopted the Jewish faith, the people did likewise as a matter of course. This illustrated the universalistic aspect of Judaism and the ubiquitous character of its people: for when this southern Russian kingdom wanted to know what Judaism was about, it was to Hasdai, a Spanish Jewish scholar and philanthropist, that they turned.

6

THE GOLDEN AGE OF JEWISH LEARNING: I

Hispano-Jewish Culture
A turning-point in the history of Spanish Jewry came about
forty years after Hasdai's death when, in 1013, a horde of
Berber invaders entered Spain from North Africa and caused
the disruption of the Caliphate with its centre at Cordova.
It was here that Jewish scholarship had especially flourished,
as can be illustrated not only from the career of Hasdai, but
from the life-story of Moses ben Enoch. Together with his
wife and son, he was on his way to Spain from the Babylonian
city of Sura, to collect funds for his academy, when he was
captured by pirates and put on board a ship engaged in slave-
trading. In despair, his wife threw herself overboard, but he
and his son reached Cordova where they were put up for
sale in the slave market. Fortunately they were seen by a
Jewish citizen who purchased them and took them to the
synagogue. In due course, the father became a leading Jewish
rabbi while the son was later appointed Nagid or 'prince' of
the Jewish community in Spain.

The Berber invasion, although it overthrew Cordova and
split the Caliphate into a number of rival kingdoms, did not
on balance adversely affect the position of the Jewish communities. It is true that there was Christian penetration from
the north, which pushed southwards and was to have catastrophic effects in succeeding centuries. But at this time the
different warring factions needed all the help they could get
in maintaining freedom and security, and this meant they
were dependent to some extent on the brains and expertise
of their more intelligent Jewish minorities. Hence, individual
Jews often rose to high positions as advisers in the state
courts. This was especially so when the states were set up by
the Berbers, some of whose ancestors may themselves have
been Jews before their conversion to Islam, and who treated
Jews with real sympathy and favour. In some cases, Jews
became army leaders — we hear, for instance, that the Battle

of Zalacea was actually postponed by mutual consent so that the Sabbath might be observed. Moreover, they came to take a leading part in the culture of this period, and became prominent in medicine, philosophy, literature and philology.

The most notable Jewish figure at the time, called by one historian the 'Admirable Crichton' of Spanish Jewry, was Samuel Ibn Nagdela (993-1055). Born of humble parents, he was forced to leave his native city, Cordova, after its seizure by the Berbers, and settled in Malaga where he opened a little spice shop, near the palace of the King of Granada's vizier. The latter came to admire his excellent calligraphy and invited him to live in Granada and become his confidential secretary. He was so successful in this role that, after the vizier's death, the king appointed him as his successor and, for a period of about twenty-five years, he virtually ruled the State. He also led its armies in battle and had the satisfaction, on one occasion, of camping with his forces on the very spot where he had slept as a starving refugee. But it was not only in leadership that he excelled. As was so typical of the Jewish ethos at its best, he combined the practical with the cultural and philanthropic. Though not a genius, he was a patron of scholarship, both Arabic and Hebraic: he wrote original compositions in imitation of the biblical books (Ecclesiastes, Proverbs and Psalms), founded a library in Granada and, through his bounty, helped poor scholars from all over the world. He became known as Samuel Ha-Nagid, and it is as Samuel the Prince that he is remembered to this day.

Greek Philosophy through Arabic Scholarship
It was not only Hebraic thought and learning that occupied the minds of Jewish scholars in this golden age of Hispano-Jewish culture. For some time past, the Arab intelligentsia had been delving into the treasures of Greek literature through newly discovered scrolls, and this had led to a fresh lease of life for the neo-Platonist school of philosophy. This was largely mystical or idealist in character, looking away from the physical and material world to an abstract, conceptual realm of absolutes. The most famous names in this context

were Plotinus and Longinus, but the Jewish philosopher Philo
of Alexandria must also be included. It was through Jewish
translations that Greek literature became known at this period
to the Christian non-Islamic world, and, hence, the oft-
repeated claim that the European Renaissance had its roots
in Jewish scholarship is by no means a fantasy.

One important subsequent development in the revival of
Greek thought had immediate consequences for all the three
great religions, Judaism, Islam and Christianity. This was the
virtual superseding of neo-Platonism by Aristotelian philosophy. What Aristotle did was to introduce the process of
induction into human thinking: that is to say, he tried to
reach ultimate truth through an objective study of physical
phenomena, and to formulate the general theories or
'causation' to which they led. This was the scientific approach
to truth and proved to be a serious challenge to the religious
outlook of both Judaism and Islam with their divine, supernatural frame of reference. Thus a tremendous area of fresh
thought was laid bare and became a new and exciting challenge
to subsequent Jewish writers through Arabic translations of
Aristotle's works.

Ibn Gabirol

But the first of the Jewish scholars we have to consider was
still under the influence of the neo-Platonic school. His name
was Solomon Ibn Gabirol and he lived at Malaga and became
the leading Jewish philosopher and poet after Hasdai. One
of his works, *Fons Vitae*, mystical and neo-Platonic in character, had a profound effect on Catholic thought and, until
the last century, was always regarded as having been written
by a Christian called Avicebron. No one dreamt that its
author was a Jew, for it expounded a metaphysical outlook
which rested on three principles, God, the world of matter
and form, and the will, which was envisaged as a kind of
intermediary between God and the material world. He also
wrote an ethical treatise called *Improvement of the Moral
Qualities*.

It is as a poet, imaginative, liturgical, and philosophical,
adapting Arabic forms to the Hebrew language, that Ibn

Gabirol left his mark on the Jewish ethos. Here are one or two examples:

From *Meditation on Life*
(Used in the Day of Atonement Memorial Service in synagogues today)

> Forget thine anguish,
>   Vexed heart, again.
> Why shouldst thou languish
> With earthly pain?
> The husk shall slumber,
>   Bedded in clay
> Silent and sombre,
>   Oblivion's prey!
> But, Spirit immortal,
> Thou at Death's portal,
>   Tremblest with fear.
> If he caress thee,
> Curse thee or bless thee,
>   Thou must draw near,
>   From him the worth of thy works to hear.
>
> Life is a vine branch;
>   A vintager, death;
> He threatens and lowers
>   More near with each breath.
> Then hasten, arise!
>   Seek God, Oh my soul!
> For time quickly flies,
>   Still far as the goal.
> Vain heart praying dumbly,
> Learn to prize humbly,
>   The meanest of fare.
> Forget all thy sorrow,
>   Behold, death is there!

(Translated by Emma Lazarus)

From *Happy He Who Saw of Old*

> Happy he who saw of old
> The high priest, with gems and gold
> All adorned from crown to hem,
> Thread thy courts, Jerusalem,
> Where the Lord's especial grace
> Ever dwelt, the centre of the whole.
>   Happy he whose eyes
>   Saw at last the cloud of glory rise,
> But to hear of it afflicts our soul.
> Happy he who saw the crowd,
> That in adoration bowed,
> As they heard the priest proclaim,
> 'One Ineffable, the Name,'
> And they answered, 'Blessed be
> God, the Lord eternally,
> He whom all created worlds extol.'
>   Happy he whose eyes
>   Saw at last the cloud of glory rise;
> But to hear of it afflicts our soul.

(Translated by Nina Davis)

After years of restless wandering, this poet and mystic died in the year 1056. Little is known of his life. He was probably an orphan, who owed the success of his literary career to the patronage of Samuel Ibn Nagdela, and somewhat of a recluse. The metaphysical and mystical quality of his writing caused him in later times to be regarded as the Hebrew Plato.

Judah Ha-Levi

During the eleventh century, a succession of Jewish moralists arose on the Spanish scene, of whom the greatest was Baḥya (*c.* 1040). He is best known for his authorship of a book called *Duties of the Heart*, which has ten divisions called 'Gates', dealing with the following subjects: God, Reflection, Worship of God, Trust in Providence, Consecration of Work, Humility, Repentance, Self-examination, the Ascetic Life, and Love of God. His style was aphoristic, as can be seen from this short extract from the Sixth Gate:

> The truly humble man will mourn for all the mistakes made by other men, and will not triumph or rejoice over them.
> Among the aids to the cultivation of humility are the contemplation of the greatness of man's obligation to the Creator . . . and on the insignificance of man in comparison with even this earth; while in comparison with the greatness of the Creator the whole universe is as nothing.

By far the most well-known of the authors who belong to this *genre* of literature was Judah Ha-Levi of Toledo (*c.* 1086-1141). He was certainly no moralist in his youth but pursued a life of gaiety and pleasure which brought him a severe rebuke from his elders. His retort might be that of any young hedonist today:

> Shall I whose years scarce number twenty-four
> Turn foe to pleasure and drink wine no more?

By profession he became a doctor and secured a wide practice in his native city. Yet the art of medicine failed to satisfy him, and, later in his life, he wrote a letter in which he complained of the long hours occupied with the 'vanity of medical science' which yet left him unable to heal the sick. During his youth he composed an important semi-philosophic work called *Al Khazari*, which is in the form of a dialogue imaginatively conducted at the court of the King of the Khazars (see above p. 59). In it, a Jewish apologist seeks to justify the Jewish faith on rational grounds and to show its superiority over pure metaphysics on the one hand and the religions of Christianity and Islam on the other.

But it was through the medium of poetry that the deepest aspirations of his soul found their genuine expression, poetry of a richly lyrical type. The language he used may be compared to that of Sappho or the *Song of Songs* — it is tender, passionate, sensuous. But though the earlier poems are erotic and express the poet's craving for an impossibly beautiful maiden, this later became sublimated, so that the loved one

is the God of Israel, and especially the land of Israel where
'the Shekhinah dwelt'. To borrow language used of that later
philosopher-poet, Spinoza, he was 'intoxicated with God and
Zion'.

Here are some samples of his poetry, though it should be
borne in mind that translation is virtually impossible and is
valuable only as indicating the poet's thinking.

To the Bridegroom
Rejoice, O young man, in thy youth,
And gather the fruit thy joy shall bear,
Thou and the wife of thy youth,
Turning now to thy dwelling to enter there.

Glorious blessings of God, who is One,
Shall come united upon thy head;
Thine house shall be at peace from dread,
Thy foes' uprising be undone,
Thou shalt lay thee down in a safe retreat;
Thou shalt rest, and thy sleep be sweet.

In thine honour, my bridegroom, prosper and live;
Let thy beauty arise and shine forth fierce;
And the heart of thine enemies God shall pierce,
And the sins of thy youth will He forgive
And bless thee in increase and all thou shalt do,
When thou settest thy hand thereto.

The Physician's Prayer
My God, heal me and I shall be healed;
Let not thine anger be kindled against me
      so that I be consumed,
My medicines are of Thee, whether good
Or evil, whether strong or weak.
It is Thou who shalt choose, not I,
Of Thy knowledge is the evil and the fair.
Not upon my power of healing I rely;
Only for Thine healing do I watch.

Ode to Zion
Thy God desired thee for a dwelling-place;
And happy is the man whom he shall choose,
And draw him nigh to rest within thy space.

Happy is he that waiteth — he shall go
To thee, and thine arising radiance see
When over him shall break thy morning glow;

And see rest for thy chosen; and sublime
Rejoicing find amid the joy of thee
Returned unto thine olden youthful time.

This passion for Zion and Jerusalem dominated his whole thought during the latter part of his life and led to a complete disillusion about the country of his birth and a yearning to visit the Holy Land.

In the East, in the East is my heart and I dwell at the end
   of the West.
How shall I join in your feasting, how shall I share in
   your jest?

He finally succeeded in satisfying his heart's desire and left Toledo (*c.* 1141) for Palestine. But a bitter disappointment lay in store for him. Far from being the city of his dreams, he found Jerusalem to be a heap of evil-smelling debris, and a constant battle-field between Moslem and Christian Crusaders. It is recorded that — such is the irony of fate — he met his end through being trampled on by an Arab horseman as he sang one of his songs of Zion by the side of her ruined wall.

7

THE GOLDEN AGE OF JEWISH LEARNING: II

Ibn Ezra

If, as has been suggested in the last chapter, Ibn Gabirol may be regarded as the Jewish Plato *par excellence*, one of the Hispano-Jewish writers of the next century, Ibn Daud (1110-80), can lay claim to be the first Jewish Aristotelian. At this period, there was a growing tendency among Jewish thinkers to grapple with the speculative, metaphysical propositions put forward by the Greek philosophers, and Ibn Daud was perhaps the first of these to approach truth from the scientific angle. He was even bold enough to identify God as the first of the Four Causes which Aristotle postulated as underlying the whole life process.

Ibn Daud's even greater contemporary, Ibn Ezra, belonged to a family of scholars and poets. Born in Spain, he travelled far and wide delivering lectures to students and being supported by some local patron in the countries where he taught. He was extremely versatile and wrote works on grammar or prosody, philosophy, and astronomy. Like his predecessor, Ibn Gabirol, he was also a great hymnologist. What marks him out from among the Jewish scholars of his own or previous ages was his totally original and revolutionary attitude to the Scriptures. This, for the first time in Jewish history, was scientific and critical in character. It was the spirit of the Bible, he taught, that emanated from heaven, not necessarily the letter. When he came across passages in the written Torah which contradicted each other, he recognized the inconsistencies and did not try to reconcile them. He even sought a natural explanation for miracles and may be regarded as the father of what is today called higher criticism.

Incidentally, Ibn Ezra was a man of considerable wit and he used this in countering the misfortunes which seemed to dog his footsteps wherever he went. He visited many countries, Italy, France and England among others, but never settled down happily in any one of them. He used to say that if he became a shroud-maker there would be no more deaths among men.

Rashi and the Tosaphists

Ibn Ezra's travels to various Jewish centres in Europe raise the important question as to whether any development in Jewish life and learning had taken place outside Spain at this period corresponding with the great Hispano-Jewish culture described above. The answer is broadly 'yes' — but with a difference. From about A.D. 1,000 a number of Franco-German Jewish schools flourished, but they concentrated largely on Talmudic scholarship and biblical exegesis. They lacked, on the whole, the deeper penetration of Spanish Jewry with its new scientific and philosophical awakening. Yet the Franco-German scholars did great service in the sphere of Jewish literary interpretation and its application to a devout religious life, and these have lasted right up to the present day.

Among the leading figures in European Jewry at this period were Rabbi Gershon and Rashi. The former founded a school at Mayence and his scholastic eminence earned for him the title 'Light of the Exile'. Unfortunately, little of his literary work remains, though we still have a hymn composed by him, a sad one, referring to the persecution of his co-religionists in the Rhineland in 1012. More important, perhaps, he is known to have drawn up a series of regulations which aimed at adapting Jewish life to the altered conditions in Europe.

The most famous of all students of the Mayence school was Rabbi Shalomo ben Isaac, known from his initials (Ra.Sh.I.) as Rashi. Born into a scholarly family, he lived for the most of his life in the little town of Troyes and brought to the tiny local Jewish community the fruit of what he had learnt in his boyhood from Rabbi Gershon and the Mayence school. He soon became the leading light of the Synagogue in biblical and talmudical exposition, and such was the clarity of his thinking that he came to be recognized as an authority on controversial matters, young students being sent to study under his personal guidance.

But what has given him a perennial ascendancy among Jewish scholars is the famous Commentary he wrote on the

Babylonian Talmud, which gave coherent shape to the vast
mass of rabbinic comment and *responsa* of which it was
composed, written as they were in a number of languages and
with a highly specialized vocabulary. Since the fall of the
Schools at Sura and Pumbeditha, this vast compendium had
become virtually unintelligible, and it was largely due to
Rashi's lucid and concise exposition that the Talmud was
transmitted as a standard work to all succeeding generations.
This applies not only to Jews: Christian scholars have made
extensive use of it, as well as of his more popular, but less
profound, commentary on the Bible. Even Martin Luther
owed a considerable debt to the scholarship of Rashi.

After his death, Rashi's characteristic work of elucidation
was carried on in a series of additions (*Tosaphot*) compiled
by a line of scholars known as Tosaphists. These were to be
found chiefly in the townships of eastern France and the
Rhineland, but, through them, Talmudists — who had never
heard of the English city — came to know of the scholars or
'wise men' of Norwich. Chief among Rashi's successors were
two of his grandsons, Samuel ben Meir and his brother Jacob
who came to be known as Rabbenu Tam, 'Our Perfect
Master'. Another famous name is that of Meir of Rothenburg,
from one of whose pupils, Asher, comes the following ethical
and humanistic teaching (Harris, *Mediaeval Jews*, p. 251):

> Be and remain grateful to anyone who hath helped thee to
> thy bread; be sincere and true with everyone, Jews and
> non-Jews; be the first to extend courteous greeting to
> everyone, whatever be his faith; provoke not to wrath one
> of another belief than thine.

Maimonides and the Culmination of Jewish Learning
One of the great issues which confronts religious thinkers in
our own day is the emergence of a comparatively new, non-
theological social philosophy known as scientific humanism.
This is based on the ancient theory going right back to the
Greek philosopher Protagoras that 'man is the measure of all
things'. No Jewish thinker or teacher would subscribe to such
a concept, for Judaism is a theistic faith. But the great figure

who now dominates the scene gained his ascendancy through his ability to combine the spirit of scientific humanism — which, as we have seen, was first developed in Spain — with that of the rabbinic scholarly research characteristic of the northern European countries, as expressed in the work of Rashi and his successors. This was Moses ben Maimon, popularly known as Maimonides, whose impact on the whole of the subsequent development of Judaism can hardly be exaggerated.

Maimonides was born in Cordova in 1135 of a family long distinguished for Jewish learning. When he was thirteen years of age he and his family suffered persecution as a result of the capture of Cordova by a section of Moslem fanatics, the Al-Mohades. Jews and Christians alike were faced with the choice of conversion to Islam or exile. Some accepted the former in its outward guise, while secretly remaining loyal to their faith. Maimon and his family decided to emigrate, first settling in Morocco, where for a time they were compelled to pay lip-service to Islam. Soon, however, they moved to Egypt where for centuries there had been a Jewish community which in the main received tolerant treatment from their Arab rulers. Here young Maimonides is said to have contributed his share towards maintaining the family by helping his brother David, a dealer in precious stones. But he studied many other things as well, including mathematics, and finally devoted himself to medicine.

It was Maimonides' medical skill that brought him in touch with a wide circle of patients, both Jewish and non-Jewish, and he finally became court physician to Saladin's vizier, who recommended him to the royal family and bestowed on him many distinctions. This was the period of the Crusades, and it was even said that he received the offer of a similar position as court physician from Richard Coeur de Lion, but was far too deeply committed to his work in Cairo to think of yet another migration. Maimonides' methods of treatment have a very modern ring about them — for he endeavoured to cure his patients by a prescribed diet before administering drugs. He led an arduous professional life, as is shown in this extract from a letter to a friend:

Do not expect to confer with me on any scientific subject for even one hour, either by day or night, for the following is my daily occupation: I dwell in Mizr (Fostat) and the Sultan resides at Kahira (Cairo); these two places are two Sabbath days' journeys (about one mile and a half) distant from each other. My duties to the Sultan are very heavy. . . . As a rule, I repair to Kahira very early in the day, and even if nothing unusual happens, I do not return to Mizr until the afternoon. Then I am almost dying with hunger; I find the ante-chambers filled with people, both Jews and Gentiles, nobles and common people, judges and bailiffs, friends and foes — a mixed multitude, who await the time of my return. I dismount from my animal, wash my hands, go forth to my patients, and entreat them to bear with me while I partake of some slight refreshment, the only meal I take in the twenty-four hours. . . Patients go in and out until nightfall, and sometimes even, I solemnly assure you, until two hours and more in the night. I converse with them, and prescribe for them while lying down from sheer fatigue; and when night falls I am so exhausted that I can scarcely speak. In consequence of this, no Israelite can have any private interview with me, except on the Sabbath. On that day the whole congregation, or, at least, the majority of the members, come to me after the morning service, when I instruct them as to their proceedings during the whole week; we study together a little until noon, when they depart. Some of them return and read with me after the afternoon service until evening prayers. In this manner I spend that day. I have related to you only a part of what you would see if you were to visit me.

Some of the noblest lines Maimonides wrote are contained in his 'physician's prayer', known as the Oath of Maimonides — which a few years ago was distributed to all British pharmacists in the form which follows:

O, God, Thy eternal providence has appointed me to watch over the life and health of Thy creatures.
May the love for my art actuate me at all times; may neither

avarice nor miserliness, nor thirst for glory, or for a great
reputation engage my mind; for the enemies of truth and
philanthropy could easily deceive me and make me forget-
ful of my lofty aim of doing good to Thy children.

May I never see in the patient anything but a fellow
creature in pain.

Grant me strength, time and opportunity always to correct
what I have acquired, always to extend its domain; for
knowledge is immense and the spirit of man can extend
infinitely to enrich itself daily with new requirements.

Today he can discover his errors of yesterday and tomorrow
he may obtain a new light on what he thinks himself sure
of today.

O, God, Thou hast appointed me to watch over the life and
death of Thy creatures; here am I ready for my vocation,
and now I turn unto my calling.

One of the extraordinary things about this dedicated
doctor is that he also found time to study and become a
recognized authority on Jewish literature and on both biblical
and talmudic teaching up to his own day. Even before he
went to Egypt he had started to write a commentary in Arabic
on the Mishnah (see p. 43) and in 1180 he produced his
Mishneh Torah or 'Repetition of the Law', written in Hebrew,
which attempted to present the great corpus of traditional
Jewish teaching in a lucid, logical form for the benefit of his
Jewish contemporaries. He summarized the basic principles
of Judaism in what became known as the 'Thirteen Articles
of Faith', and though these were never officially accepted by
any rabbinical synod, they came to be regarded as an authoritative exposition of Jewish belief and were later incorporated
in the Jewish prayer-book. Taken from the Authorized Daily
Prayer Book (p. 93), they are as follows:

1.   I believe with perfect faith that the Creator, blessed
be his name, is the Author and Guide of everything that
has been created, and that he alone has made, does make,
and will make all things.

2.   I believe with perfect faith that the Creator, blessed
be his name, is a Unity, and that there is no unity in any

manner like unto his, and that he alone is our God, who was, is, and will be.

3. I believe with perfect faith that the Creator, blessed be his name, is not a body, and that he is free from all accidents of matter, and that he has not any form whatsoever.

4. I believe with perfect faith that the Creator, blessed be his name, is the first and the last.

5. I believe with perfect faith that to the Creator, blessed be his name, and to him alone, it is right to pray, and that it is not right to pray to any being besides him.

6. I believe with perfect faith that all the words of the prophets are true.

7. I believe with perfect faith that the prophecy of Moses our teacher, peace be unto him, was true, and that he was the chief of the prophets, both of those that preceded and those that followed him.

8. I believe with perfect faith that the whole Law, now in our possession, is the same that was given to Moses our teacher, peace be unto him.

9. I believe with perfect faith that this Law will not be changed, and that there will never be any other law from the Creator, blessed be his name.

10. I believe with perfect faith that the Creator, blessed be his name, knows every deed of the children of men, and all their thoughts, as it is said, It is he that fashioneth the hearts of them all, that giveth heed to their deeds.

11. I believe with perfect faith that the Creator, blessed be his name, rewards those that keep his commandments, and punishes those that transgress them.

12. I believe with perfect faith in the coming of the Messiah, and, though he tarry, I will wait daily for his coming.

13. I believe with perfect faith that there will be a resurrection of the dead at the time when it shall please the Creator, blessed be his name, and exalted be the remembrance of him for ever and ever.

It is not only within the Jewish community that Maimonides

is of such great stature, but to the cause of religion and the development of theological thought in general. Through his reinterpretation of Judaism in the light of Aristotelian philosophy and his efforts to give a rational basis for divine revelation and faith, he exerted a profound influence on Christian theologians, and contemporary Christian philosophers such as Thomas Aquinas readily acknowledged the debt they owed to him. He was, in fact, amazingly tolerant of other religions and once wrote of Christianity, 'It has done more to spread abroad the Bible than Judaism itself; whereever it carried trade it carried the Bible, doing Jewish work with non-Jewish hands.'

The book in which this special genius of his found its completest expression was the last he wrote: *Moreh Nevukhim* or 'Guide for the Perplexed'. It is here, above all, in what might be described as his masterpiece, that he attempted to reconcile reason and faith and build a bridge between natural law and divine agency. Here, too, the Golden Age of Jewish learning reached its zenith, and no more fitting conclusion can be given to this account of its development than the following two extracts from Maimonides' *summum opus*:

There is a great difference between the knowledge which the producer of a thing possesses concerning it, and the knowledge which other persons possess concerning the same thing. Suppose a thing is produced in accordance with the knowledge of the producer, the producer was then guided by his knowledge in the act of producing the thing. Other people, however, who examine this work and acquire a knowledge of the whole of it, depend for that knowledge on the work itself. E.g., An artisan makes a box in which weights move with the running of the water, and thus indicate how many hours have passed of the day and of the night. The whole quantity of the water that is to run out, the different ways in which it runs, every thread that is drawn, and every little ball that descends — all this is fully perceived by him who makes the clock; and his knowledge is not the result of observing the movements as they are actually going on; but, on the contrary, the movements are produced in accordance with his knowledge. But another person who looks at that instrument will receive fresh knowledge at every movement he perceives; the longer he looks on, the more knowledge does he acquire; he will gradually increase his knowledge till he fully understands the machinery. If an infinite number of movements were assumed for this instrument, he would never be able to complete his knowledge. Besides, he cannot know any of the movements before they take place, since he only knows them from their actual occurrence. The same is the case with every object, and its relation to our knowledge and God's knowledge of it. Whatever we know of the things is derived from observation; on that account it is impossible for us to know that which will take place in future, or that which is infinite.

(*Guide for the Perplexed*, trs. M. Friedlander, Part 3, ch. 21)

Again, his great passage on intelligence and the imaginative faculty:

It is necessary to consider the nature of the divine influence which enables us to think, and gives us the various degrees of intelligence. For this influence may reach a person only in a small measure, and in exactly the same proportion would then be his intellectual condition, whilst it may reach another person in such a measure that, in addition to his own perfection, he can be the means of perfection for others. The same relation may be observed throughout the whole Universe. There are some beings so perfect that they can govern other beings, but there are also beings that are only perfect in so far as they can govern themselves and cannot influence other beings. In some cases the influence of the (Active) Intellect reaches only the logical and not the imaginative faculty; either on account of the insufficiency of that influence, or on account of a defect in the constitution of the imaginative faculty and the consequent condition of wise men or philosophers. If, however, the imaginative faculty is naturally in the most perfect condition, this influence may, as has been explained by us and

by other philosophers, reach both his logical and his imaginative faculties: this is the case with prophets. But it
happens sometimes that the influence only reaches the
imaginative faculty on account of the insufficiency of the
logical faculty, arising either from a natural defect, or from
a neglect in training. This is the case with statesmen, law-
givers, diviners, charmers, and men that have true dreams,
or do wonderful things by strange means or secret arts,
though they are not wise men; all these belong to the third
class. It is further necessary to understand that some persons belonging to the third class perceive scenes, dreams,
and confused images, when awake, in the form of a
prophetic vision. They then believe that they are prophets;
they wonder that they perceive visions, and think that
they have acquired wisdom without training. They fall into
grave errors as regards important philosophical principles,
and see a strange mixture of true and imaginary things.
All this is the consequence of the strength of their imaginative faculty, and the weakness of their logical faculty, which
has not developed, and has not passed from potentiality
to actuality.

(*Guide for the Perplexed*, Part 2, ch. 37)

8

PERSECUTION AND THE GHETTO LIFE

The Crusades
Maimonides died in 1204 in Fostat in Egypt (see letter to his
friend, p. 72), and such was the honour in which he was
held that a general fast was proclaimed in Jerusalem to com-
memorate the passing of Jewry's greatest scholar. A proverb
even became current in Jewish circles lasting to our own
time: 'From Moses (the Law-Giver) unto Moses (Maimonides)
there has been none like unto Moses.' But, sad to relate, the
period that followed his death was one of the darkest in the
history of his people and can only be paralleled by the
terrible chapter which started with Hitler's rise to power in
1933.

The cloud gathered over Europe shortly before Maimonides
was born, in the shape of the First Crusade. The motives
behind this, as well as the subsequent development of the
movement, are part of general history, but severe repercussions
were felt by the scattered Jewish communities. The prime
object of the Crusades, following interference with Christian
pilgrimage to the Holy Places by Moslem fanatics, was to
rescue Jerusalem and the Holy Sepulchre from Moslem control. This was regarded as a sacred task. but unfortunately
the argument did not stop there. In the course of their march
through Europe to liberate the Holy Land and the tomb of
Jesus, the Crusaders found themselves passing the settlements
of those whose ancestors, they firmly believed, had crucified
him. Should they not begin by exterminating such infidels as
a prelude to this sacred task?

So it came about that, for four centuries after the First
Crusade of 1096, the Jews of Europe were ceaselessly harried,
suffering all the agonies of expulsion and persecution. There
were wholesale massacres of the Jewish populations at Speyer,
Worms, Mayence, Metz and other European cities. Sometimes
the alternative of baptism was offered — but rarely accepted.
The whole community of Jews at Worms, for instance, are

said to have died with the *Shema* on their lips ('Hear, O Israel: the Lord our God, the Lord is One').

There were some incidents, however, which threw occasional gleams of light on this scene of almost total darkness. On occasion there were interventions, in the diocese or town where they held authority, by individual prelates or governors, animated by the true Christian spirit of pity for the oppressed. During the First Crusade, two bishops, those of Speyer and Cologne, did their best to save the local Jewish communities from annihilation. Later, in the Second Crusade, Bernard of Clairvaux, though a pioneer of the Crusading movement as a whole, used all his eloquence to prevent these orgies of cruelty against the Jews. Yet, sad to relate, most mediaeval Christian historians tended to explain such acts of humaneness as being prompted by Jewish bribery.

Persecution of the Jews and Albigenses

It was not only the Crusading movement, however, that brought about Jewish persecution in the Middle Ages. Another motive was the perennial need of mediaeval monarchs for money to finance their wars and other operations. In this, they found their Jewish minorities an easy source of exploitation, and a good illustration of this can be drawn from our own country. Here the king became the legal 'owner' of all English Jews who were compelled, through the process of lending money to local borrowers at an exorbitant rate of interest, to pay large sums into the royal treasury. As their profits through this altogether irrational process declined, they became less and less useful to the reigning monarch, and in 1290, when almost the last ounce had been squeezed out of them, they were ruthlessly expelled from this country by Edward I.

Two other causes of widespread Jewish persecution were the Black Death and the ritual murder slander. From 1348 to 1351, Europe was ravaged by the plague, the common explanation of which was that the Jews had poisoned the drinking-wells. In the superstitious panic which swept across Europe during those years, nobody questioned how, if that were so, Jews themselves could have survived. It was simply noted that they did survive, and this was attributed to magic arts. It was, in fact, almost certainly due to the superior habits of Jewish hygiene, sanitation, and diet. Much later, in 1394, Charles VI of France expelled the Jews from that country as a result of these accusations. By the irony of fate, the edict giving them six weeks' notice was published on 17 September, the Jewish festival of *Yom Kippur* — the Day of Atonement, which is the most solemn day of repentance and mourning in the Jewish calendar.

The allegations of ritual murder were of two types. The first imputed to the Jews the murder of a Christian child in preparation for the Passover festival: his blood was said to have been used in the manufacture of *Matzos*, the unleavened bread used during the Passover. The second followed the acceptance of the doctrine of transubstantiation by the fourth Lateran Council in 1215. It was said that the Jews periodically purloined a piece of the consecrated Host and, by using 'the blood of Christ' as an ingredient of the *Matzos*, they re-enacted the crucifixion. Fantastic as such allegations were, they brought untold misery to the mediaeval Jewish communities. We have but to read the stories of various supposed Christian martyrs such as William of Norwich and Hugh of Lincoln (famous in literature as the hero of Chaucer's 'Prioress' Tale'), to realize the lengths to which false legends can be carried. It is only of recent years that a plaque has been displayed in Lincoln Cathedral which states explicitly that the story of Hugh of Lincoln has no historical foundation.

When totalitarian patterns of thought begin to dominate Church or State, it is not only the minority group which suffers but all those who try to preserve independent minds and refuse to conform to the establishment. Thus, there had grown up in Provence a sect of heretical Christians who believed that the material world and matter were evil, the dominion of the evil spirit. Human souls, they contended, were spirits imprisoned in material flesh, only to be freed by extreme ascetic practices. This sect was called the Catharans (*Cathari*, the pure), or, more locally, the Albigenses, from the town of Albi where they were numerous. The Albigenses were friendly to the Jews, and it was popularly (though erroneously) thought that their doctrines were influenced by Judaism. The movement therefore stimulated the Church's animosity against the Jews at the close of the twelfth century and, during the suppression of the sect, many Jews were massacred.

In 1207, for instance, Pope Innocent III called for a Crusade against the Albigenses. It was led by a fanatical monk, Arnold of Cîteaux, 'who spared neither dignity nor sex nor age' (as he wrote to the Holy Father) and who managed by 1228 to put an end to the whole Albigensian movement in Provence and the freedom of religious thought for which it had stood. A similar instance of Christian martyrdom at the hands of Christians took place two centuries later when John Hus, of Prague, started a movement against Church corruption and, being accused of 'Judaizing', was burnt at the stake in 1415. It was through such independent liberalizing spirits as these that the great Reformation movement eventually took place.

Inquisition and the Marranos
The saddest chapter for Jews in the history of mediaeval Europe relates to the country where for centuries they had lived happily and indeed prosperously — the Spanish peninsula. The change in their fortunes began when, in 1230, the Christian kingdom of Castile united with Leon and its power gradually spread over other towns in what had hitherto been Moslem Spain, such as Cordova and Seville. Henceforth, tolerance of Jews and other non-Christians began to decline. Through the influence of the Friars a series of anti-Jewish riots took place, and Jews had to choose between baptism and death: it is said that in this way a fanatical Dominican friar, Vicente Ferrer, secured the conversion of no less than 35,000 Jews.

Here an important distinction must be made between genuine Christian converts, and those who, under compulsion, accepted the outward forms of Christian practice and worship in order to save their lives, though inwardly remaining loyal to their own faith which they continued to practise in secret. The latter came to be called Marranos (the mediaeval Spanish for 'swine') and they played an important part in subsequent

Jewish history. By continuing to observe the Passover in their cellars and singing Sabbath hymns quietly behind closed doors and windows, they succeeded in preserving the great Jewish heritage and bequeathing it to their children.

This kind of surreptitious preservation of one's religion is a common phenomenon shared by all persecuted sects but one which, in the Spanish scene, led to fearful consequences. In 1469 Isabella, sister of Henry IV of Castile, married Ferdinand of Aragon, and the marriage brought about the unification of Christian Spain. Isabella, devout and high-minded, was by far the more attractive of this ruthless pair of rulers, but both were determined to subjugate the nobles, to overcome the Moorish kingdoms, and to achieve a religious as well as a political unity which would be incomplete while Jews remained in the country. There had been an Inquisition for many years, a court of inquiry to root out Christian heresy, but it had no jurisdiction over non-Christian faiths such as Judaism and Islam. In the period 1477-90, therefore, in spite of opposition, Ferdinand and Isabella founded the Supreme Council of the Inquisition, dependent entirely on themselves and making 'purity of blood' essential for both clerical and lay office. This new Inquisition was aimed specifically at the Jewish Marranos.

The Inquisition adopted the most ruthless methods of extermination and when, in 1483, Torquemada — probably himself of Jewish extraction — became Inquisitor-General, the infamous *auto-da-fé* ('act of faith') came to be the normal instrument for carrying out its decisions. According to its procedure, the unbeliever was dressed in a flame-coloured robe, carried a cross forced into his hands, was led to the *Quemadoro* (place of burning), there listened to a sermon, and was finally burnt at the stake in front of king, queen and a large crowd of the populace. Yet even this policy, however ruthless, failed to achieve its objective, and there were still some Jews in Spain who refused, in spite of every threat, to renounce their faith and managed not only to profess it openly but to rescue and give hiding to many of the Marranos: an inconsistency — or lack of thoroughness — even in the viciousness of such an institution as the Inquisition, but probably attributable to the wealth and position of certain powerful Jews. So, in 1492, at the instigation of Torquemada, Ferdinand and Isabella issued a decree banishing all unbaptized Jews from Spain. They did this in spite of the remonstrance of a leading Jew at the court called Isaac Abravanel, who had become what today we would call Chancellor of the Exchequer; and such was the prevailing fanaticism that there was a plot to steal and baptize his baby grandson in order to force him to renounce his people's cause. Probably the determining factor in Ferdinand's decision was the prospect of enormous gain for his treasury which would come from the property of the expelled Jewish community. All Jews, unless prepared to renounce their religion and become converts to Christianity, were ordered to leave Spain, taking no property with them. This decree, of March 1492, brought to an end a glorious chapter of Jewish history.

The Kimḥis of Provence

A considerable time before this, certain internal developments had taken place among the Jewish communities, which were partly the result of persecution. As we have seen, the Golden Age of Jewry in Spain had produced an outflowing of the Jewish spirit which found expression in some of the most original and creative literature of all time. This now gave way to an interest in the lesser, yet significant, illuminations of grammar, philology and translation. Two Jewish families of the Provence showed remarkable expertise in these subjects: the Kimḥis of Narbonne and the Tibbons of Lunel.

Joseph Kimḥi, in the twelfth century, was the first writer to bring Spanish culture into France and to some extent he anticipated Ibn Ezra in transplanting the scientific thinking of the Judaeo-Arab world to Christian Europe. His more famous son, David Kimḥi (1160-1235), taught Hebrew to both Jews and Christians through his Biblical Dictionary (*Sepher ha-Shorashim*: 'Book of Roots') and his Grammar, while his popular presentation of Ibn Ezra's grammatical work – as well as his philosophical and biblical commentaries, later translated into Latin – had a far-reaching effect on theological scholarship.

Judah Ibn Tibbon was forced by persecution to leave his birthplace in Granada in 1150, and settled in Lunel, where he became known as 'the father of translators'. He produced Hebrew versions of many works originally written in Arabic, including Bahya's *Duties of the Heart* and Judah Ha-Levi's *The Khazar*. His son, Samuel, an even better scholar than his father, translated Aristotle's works from their Arabic form into Hebrew, as well as Maimonides' great book, *Guide to the Perplexed*.

Anti-Maimonist Movement

This translation of Maimonides' book into Hebrew, from the original Arabic in which it was written, enabled the book to become available to the scattered Jewish communities of Europe, but its rationalistic philosophic approach caused the same kind of ferment to arise in Jewry as that in earlier years between the Rabbanites and Karaites (see p. 55). It may be said of Judaism, as well as of other religions such as Christianity, that the faith which it embodies, based on a belief in divine revelation (in the former case through the Torah), carries within itself an inevitable dichotomy. There is, firstly, the mystical, fundamentalist school of thought which regards the holy scriptures as the literal word of God and as possessing divine authority for all human contingencies — in the case of Judaism, the Bible and Mishnah. Secondly, there is the more rationalistic, critical, less emotional outlook which views the 'written word' as a human medium through which divine inspiration has permeated, but which itself is, therefore, open to modification and adaptation in conformity with later scientific and intellectualist trends. There is, among modern theologians, a divergence which runs precisely along these lines, and it was this internal dichotomy that rent the Jewish people as the result of Maimonides' rationalistic line of approach.

The dispute was carried on with extreme bitterness on both sides. It spread to all the centres of Jewish learning in Europe and led to the fiercest denunciations, invective and even to excommunication. The anti-Maimonists went to the length of appealing to the Inquisition for support, but when this tribunal ordered Maimonides' writings and, later, the Talmud to be burnt, it put an end to open conflict, and the schism, henceforth, became an internal one.

One of the leaders of the anti-Maimonists was Nahmanides (1194-1270) who, though he accepted rabbinical teaching without question, was a less severe, more mystical, and more humane man than his austere, uncompromising contemporaries. He did great service to Judaism as a whole by emphasizing the joyous quality inherent in its practice and, although he rejected the total philosophic approach to truth of Aristotle — accepting the demands of Halakhic authority — he nevertheless stressed the importance of Haggadah (see p. 45) as a medium of religious teaching and experience through metaphor, symbol and homily.

At this time there took place a number of theological debates between representatives of the Christian Church and the Jews and, in a famous 'Disputation' at Barcelona in 1263, it was Nahmanides who defended Judaism. The Christian protagonist who now publicly challenged Nahmanides in debate, and who had already encountered him on a previous occasion, was an apostate Jew, Pablo Christiani. Converted from Judaism, Christiani had become a Dominican and was a violent anti-Jewish agitator and propagandist. In the course of his defence — held before King James I of Aragon as arbiter — Nahmanides made the following points:

1. 'The coming of the Messiah' (around which the discussion was waged) 'has not the doctrinal importance for the Jew that it has for the Christian. (To the latter he is a Saviour and Divinity, to the former a human king.)'

2. 'The Talmudic Haggadah' (on which Christiani expected to score most of his points) 'are only homilies, moral lessons, parables, ideas of God's dealing told in simple metaphors, and therefore they carry no authority of doctrine or of law.'

3. 'As the merit of religious fidelity is proportioned to the sacrifice entailed, therefore it is more meritorious, just because it is harder, for the Jews to live loyally to their faith under a Christian ruler than under their own Messiah

in their own land.'

(Harris, Mediaeval Jews, p. 218)

Naḥmanides' own account of the disputation shows him to have exhibited courage as well as humour — as he did again on the following Sabbath when he replied to the King's conversionist address in the Synagogue. Although he had been promised immunity, Naḥmanides was tried for blasphemy, and the Dominicans unhappily succeeded in securing his expulsion from Spain. He passed his last years in Palestine.

The Flight Eastwards

The wholesale expulsion of Jews from the western countries of Europe as the result of the Crusades, the Inquisition or — as in the case of England — a blend of religious and economic factors led them to seek refuge in eastern European countries, particularly Poland and Turkey. Poland was economically a primitive country whose population consisted of a few noble families and a mass of serfs who tilled the soil or worked in simple industries. There was no middle or commercial class, and the Jewish refugees supplied just such a need. For this reason, they had been welcomed in the country as far back as the tenth century when the remnant of the Khazars (see p. 59) settled there. It was perhaps due to the fact that the Church was less organized in Poland than elsewhere that the attempts to suppress them or restrict their opportunities were ignored and their legal status was confirmed. In 1264 they were even given a charter of self-government in relation to their civil and religious life, while under Casimir III (1310-70) they were accorded freedom of residence, equal taxation and the right to hold property. Casimir, in his opposition to the nobles, earned the title of 'King of the Serfs and Jews'; murder of a Jew was punishable by death, and on one occasion the king addressed them as 'our dear and faithful subjects'. It is not surprising that, in spite of many ups and downs shared with the general population of that distressful country, the Jewish community in Poland has held a unique position in the preservation of Judaism and provided a centre of Jewish learning right up to the days of the Nazi invasion.

There is no space, here, to describe the varying fortunes

which befell Jewish immigrants in other countries such as Portugal and Rumania, though mention will be made later of their position in Italy and England. But an exception must be made with regard to Turkey, to which many Jews fled after the expulsion from Spain. The Turks had established a powerful dynasty in succession to the Byzantine Empire after their capture of Constantinople in 1453. They were a Moslem power and as such accorded refuge to Jewish emigrants from Christian countries, generously accepting refugees from Spain and Portugal. The Turkish Jewish community, predominantly Sephardi (Spanish), became of great importance. Jews were favoured partly as a trading element and partly as a counter-balance to the Christian minorities in Turkey. Certain families acquired both wealth and influence, notably the Nasi family, of which Joseph Nasi, a Marrano from Portugal, became the friend of Selim, the heir to the throne. Given the lease of Tiberias, in Palestine, Nasi attempted to plant there a colony of expatriated European Jews — a not entirely successful venture. On Selim's accession, he became the most powerful person in the state and was created Duke of Naxos. Later, Nasi was promised the crown of Cyprus, being partly responsible for the conquest of that island by the Turks, but was not, in the event, given this distinction.

Joseph Caro (1488-1575), a Jew whose family had wandered from Spain to settle eventually in Constantinople, was also active in Palestine, founding a *Yeshivah*, or school, in the town of Safed (see chapter 4, p. 50).

Sephardim and Ashkenazim

One curious by-product of the settlement of mediaeval Jewish communities in different parts of Europe, and their subsequent drift to other countries, was a division which arose between those from the Spanish peninsula and those whose background was rooted in more eastern countries such as Germany and Poland. The former were called Sephardim from a supposed biblical name for Spain: the latter, Ashkenazim, similarly from a Hebrew word denoting Germany. The Spanish and Portuguese retained the more aristocratic habits and culture of the countries from which they came and tended to

look down on their less-cultured brethren from the East —
taking over some of the intolerance from which they
themselves had suffered, and refusing to worship with Ashkenazi Jews or to intermarry with them. The Ashkenazi Jews,
following the Crusades, tended to migrate eastwards in Europe,
in later times passing back to western Europe and from there
to America. In the Middle Ages, they were roughly equal in
numbers to the Sephardim but, just before 1933, they constituted some nine-tenths of the Jewish people (about
15,000,000 out of 16,500,000). After the holocaust of 1939-
45, the proportion became some 9,500,000 out of 11,500,000.

The ritual and language distinctions between the two groups
have lasted right up to the present day, but in recent times
have ceased to have any social significance. There is some
difference in liturgy and the pronunciation of Hebrew, as any
Londoner can tell by attending services at, say, the Bevis
Marks (Sephardi) and the Central (Ashkenazi) Synagogues.
The Ashkenazi ritual tends to be nearer to the ancient
Palestinian tradition. Until the twentieth century, the overwhelming majority of Ashkenazi Jews spoke Yiddish, and a
good many still do. This is a hybrid language, half Hebrew,
half German in origin, the *lingua franca* of the Jews of
Eastern Europe. Sephardi Jews, on the other hand, used a
Judaeo-Spanish dialect called *Ladino*, the basis of which was
mainly mediaeval Castilian with many Hebrew words, and
which was written in Hebrew. It was spoken along the
Mediterranean and is still used in Israel and a few other
centres such as Turkey.

Life in the Ghetto

Not all Jews at this period moved eastwards to Poland or
Turkey, for many of them lacked initiative or even the will
to uproot themselves from countries which for centuries had
been their homelands in spite of the persecution they had had
to endure. Gradually, however, in almost all Christian countries
they were separated from the rest of the population and
forced to live in ghettos, a word probably derived from
Getto, the gun-foundry in Venice bordering the Jewish quarter.
Originally, at the time of the Exile, these separations had

been voluntary (they still are in some towns today, due to the natural desire to live near or around a synagogue and to carry out the Jewish way of life with all the customs, such as observance of the dietary laws, which this entails). But segregation, which was implicit in Church legislation of the twelfth century, gradually became reinforced following pressure from the Friars in Italy. In 1555, Pope Paul IV ordered that Jews in the Papal State should live in separated areas. This became the rule throughout Italy, and the Italian 'ghetto' became the more or less universal term used in this context — varied by *Judengasse* ('Jew's alley') or *Judenstadt* ('Jew's town'). Jews were crowded into the most squalid quarters of the big towns, surrounded by high walls — which did not prevent marauding mobs entering from outside. They were forced to wear a special badge, and were denied any social relationship with their fellow-citizens. In addition, they were restricted in trade, and prevented from becoming craftsmen owing to their exclusion from Christian guilds. Membership of such guilds meant, of necessity, participation in Christian ritual, which would automatically exclude a Jew. Moreover, not content with such exclusion, the Christian guilds made every attempt to limit the practice of their trades to Christians alone. Living conditions can be illustrated by the case of the ghetto at Frankfurt-on-Main. Here four thousand people were packed into fewer than two hundred houses in a dark and narrow street, so that two or even three families had to live in one room. In Rome, the ghetto was frequently flooded by the waters of the Tiber which left thick layers of mud and a stench which were a constant source of contagion and disease.

The one solace of these ghetto communities, the one haven of refuge, was the Jewish home-life with its warm, radiant and gracious atmosphere, and especially the Sabbath observance with its weekly reminder of God's love for his people. The candles, white cloth, sanctification over bread and wine, the praise of the wife (Prov. 31.10-31), the blessing of children and the Sabbath hymns — all these ushered in the observance each Friday night. Here are some verses from the inaugural hymn (composed *c.* 1550) which, in contrast to the squalor of all the ghetto life, symbolizes the Sabbath as a bride entering her home:

Come, my friend, to meet the bride; let us welcome the presence of the Sabbath.

'Observe' and 'Remember the Sabbath day,' the only God caused us to hear in a single utterance: the Lord is One, and his name is One to his renown and his glory and his praise. *(Come, etc.)*

Come, let us go to meet the Sabbath, for it is a well-spring of blessing; from the beginning, from of old it was ordained — last in production, first in thought. *(Come, etc.)*

O sanctuary of our King, O regal city, arise, go forth from thy overthrow; long enough hast thou dwelt in the valley of weeping; verily He will have compassion upon thee. *(Come, etc.)*

Shake thyself from the dust, arise, put on the garments of thy glory, O my people! Through the son of Jesse, the Bethlehemite, draw Thou nigh unto my soul, redeem it. *(Come, etc.)*

Arouse thyself, arouse thyself, for thy light is come: arise, shine; awake, awake; give forth a song; the glory of the Lord is revealed upon thee. *(Come, etc.)*

Be not ashamed, neither be confounded. Why art thou cast down, and why art thou disquieted? The poor of my people trust in thee, and the city shall be builded on her own mound. *(Come, etc.)*

And they that spoil thee shall be a spoil, and all that would swallow thee shall be far away: thy God shall rejoice over thee, as a bridegroom rejoiceth over his bride. *(Come, etc.)*

Thou shalt spread abroad on the right hand and on the left, and thou shalt reverence the Lord. Through the offspring of Perez we also shall rejoice and be glad. *(Come, etc.)*

Come in peace, thou crown of thy husband, with rejoicing and with cheerfulness, in the midst of the faithful of the chosen people: come, O bride; come, O bride.

Come, my friend, to meet the bride; let us welcome the presence of the Sabbath.

It was this kind of joyous religious ceremonial that prevented the breaking of the Jewish spirit during the long stifling years of ghetto life, and which kept their Messianic hopes alive. Perez, incidentally, was the ancestor of King David, who was descended from him through Boaz, the husband of Ruth.

9

JEWISH MYSTICISM

The Internal Effects of Persecution

Consideration must now be given to the ways in which the forceful restraint and physical persecution described in the last chapter affected Jewish religious thought and practice during the following centuries. One of the lessons which has been slowly and painfully learnt through man's long experience in history is that original thinking and expression require a free atmosphere, and that where compulsive systems prevail, as in the mediaeval ghetto, the range of spiritual development is seriously circumscribed. This is precisely what happened in the Jewish scene at the end of their Golden Age.

The Jewish communities in Europe, because of the restrictions discussed in the last chapter, were thrown in on themselves and, as so often happens in these circumstances, the forces of reaction set in. A new 'fence round the Law' was erected and the bold, scientific, progressive outlook frowned upon. When a scholar like Elijah Levita (c. 1468-1549) taught that the Hebrew Masoretic text of the Bible was a late edition and not the work of Moses Ibn Ezra, he roused his fellow Jews in France to fury. He even had to fall back on Christian support and, of one of his Christian pupils, Cardinal Egidio of Viterbo, he writes:

> I swear by my Creator that a certain Christian, Cardinal Egidio, my pupil for ten years, came to me and kissed me saying 'Blessed be the God of the universe who has brought thee hither. Now abide with me and be my teacher, and I shall be to thee as a father and support thee in my house and bear all thy wants.' Thus we took counsel together, 'iron sharpening iron'. I imparted my spirit to him and learned from him excellent and valuable things that are in accordance with truth.

Another scholar of this period, Azariah dei Rossi (c. 1511-78) had to face something like excommunication when he questioned the reliability of the Talmud and tried to make known among his contemporaries the Apocryphal writings and the philosophy of Philo. His writings were, in some rabbinical quarters, forbidden to readers under the age of twenty-five.

This development found its positive expression in a number of attempts to codify the Oral Law and in this way win back the total acceptance of Talmudic authority. The process had started as early as the eleventh century with a digest composed by Rabbi Alfasi, who lived and taught at Fez in North Africa — hence his name, Al-Fasi, 'man of Fez'. We have seen, too, in a previous chapter how Maimonides sought to summarize and clarify the Oral Law in his *Mishneh Torah*. But now it was to achieve something like a final consummation. In 1564-5, Joseph Caro, a Spanish Jew who had settled first in Constantinople and then in Safed, a town of Galilee, compiled his *Shulhan Arukh* ('The Prepared Table' — see p. 50), a massive codification of Talmudic laws and rabbinic *responsa*, extending from the time when the Mishnah was produced up to his own day.

This became the authoritative code for Judaism, and has remained so in the case of Orthodox Judaism right up to our own time. Even today, if a Rabbinic Court is consulted about some question of Jewish law, practice or ethics, instead of having to carry out the almost impossible task of reading right through the untidy, endless mass of Talmudical writings, it can quickly find firm and precise answers in the *Shulhan Arukh*. Yet, as is always the case with written codes of law, the binding authority it established had its dangers as well as its advantages. It meant in practice that, although a unity ensuring agreement as to what Jewish law demands was accepted throughout the Jewish diaspora, its officially recognized position had, in some extreme quarters, a cramping effect, preventing the free growth, development and adaptation which were essential to the whole concept of Torah. This danger, however, by no means nullifies its great achievement, which was to preserve the unity and integrity of the Jewish people.

Jewish Mysticism (Kabbalah)

As well as the legalism described in the last paragraph, there
was another development in many Jewish circles which arose
from persecution and the restricted ghetto life: this was a
tendency to emphasize the mystical element in Judaism.
Mysticism is, to some extent, escapist. It helps the mind to
transcend not only the restraints of legalism and the forms of
religious discipline, but also the physical barriers of an oppressive state of authority. We have seen that, in the case of
mediaeval Jewry, this tendency started with the protest of
Naḥmanides, but its roots go much further back in the total
history of Jewish religious thought.

There is, first, a great deal in the Bible itself which was, or
came to be regarded as, allegorical in character. Some of the
early stories in Genesis, such as those of the Creation — of
which there are two accounts, deriving perhaps from Babylonian sources — came to have a mystical interpretation. The
visions of the prophets, such as Ezekiel's of the four chariots,
gave rise to imaginative speculation; even a love story like
that of the Song of Solomon came to be regarded as an
allegory of God's love for Israel. We have also seen how this
mystical element in scripture influenced the great Alexandrian
philosopher, Philo, and the Gnostic movement. A parallel in
the development of Greek thought can be found in the
whole neo-Platonic school of philosophy.

In the Jewish context, these mystical writings came to be
summarized under the term *Kabbalah*, which really means
tradition, and they had a tremendous vogue between the
thirteenth and sixteenth centuries. At their best, as we shall
see, they took the Kingdom of God by storm and provided a
bridge, through poetry and myth, over which the humblest
worshipper could approach the presence of his Creator and
feel himself to be a part of the universal mind. But the whole
of this mystical outlook had its obverse side and was fraught
with serious danger. It tended to confuse truth with wildest
fancy. One of its methods, for example, was based on the fact
that Hebrew letters are also numerals, and it was presumed
that there was some mystical relation between them. An
instance of this is provided by the claim that a boy's

confirmation (*Bar Mitzvah*) at the age of thirteen rests on divine authority, because the numerical value of the letters making up the Hebrew word *Echad* (which emphasizes the central doctrine of God's unity) amounted to thirteen. All kinds of magical ideas, including belief in demons, angels, incantation, the evil eye and so on, took their place in the Kabbalistic tradition, side by side with some of the sublimest concepts of the divine in the whole of religious thought. Such a mystical development, of course, is not peculiar to Judaism, but is also found, though in different forms, embedded in Christianity.

The Zohar

Both these elements, the sublime and the crudely super-stitious, are to be found in a work which appeared in the latter part of the thirteenth century, called the *Zohar* ('Splendour'). It was written, or at least compiled, by a saintly Spanish scholar called Moses ben Leon who was steeped in the mystical literature of the Hebrews as well as that of other religions. He claimed that his book had been written centuries ago by one of the Tannaitic rabbis (see p. 44), that he had just discovered it and that therefore it had the same binding force as the Talmud itself. This, it may be said in passing, was a frequent device in early times, and not unknown at the present day, through which an author sought to get something like divine authority for his own composition.

Partly through this device, partly owing to its intrinsic merit, the *Zohar* gained immense prestige among mediaeval Jewry. That it was of late date is certain, for it refers to events which took place long after the Talmudic period and drew not only from the Bible and the Talmud, but from Persian and Hindu sources as well. But its universal and mystical character supplied just what many people were thirsting for, and its influence extended well beyond the ghetto walls or the narrow confines of the Jewish communities. It was closely studied by Christian scholars and, as we shall see in a later chapter, supplied patterns of thought which were accepted by the Christian Apocalyptists and so were instrumental in producing the Reformation. But like other

Kabbalistic literature it had the defects of its qualities. It
could rise to such sayings as, 'A man should so live that at
the close of every day he can repeat: I have not wasted my
day' and 'When man is at one, God is one'. But much of it
dealt in the crudest fashion with verbal subtleties of all kinds
and drew far-fetched allegorical interpretations from the
chance arrangements of the biblical text.

False Messiahs

One result of the Kabbalistic movement, with its escapist
tendency and indulgence in ecstatic hopes and wish-fulfilment,
was a new concentration on Messianism. Ever since the downfall of Bar Kokhba, the Jewish people had looked for a
heaven-sent deliverer who, in accordance with ancient prophecy, would redeem his people from darkness and oppression
and usher in an era of peace and happiness for the whole of
mankind. This was particularly marked from the time of the
Crusades and, again, between the thirteenth and sixteenth
centuries, with their recourse to magic, superstition and a
belief in divine intervention. Throughout this time, there
arose a number of pseudo-Messiahs who claimed, and were
often believed, to be the awaited 'Messenger of God'.

The most notable among them were David Reubeni,
Solomon Molcho, David Alroy and finally Shabbetai Tzevi,
and the stories of their meteoric careers make strange and
almost unbelievable reading in our rational, scientific age.
Reubini, for instance, who lived from about 1490 to 1535,
was nothing more than a quick-witted adventurer. He managed
to persuade his supporters to escort him, riding on a white
horse, to the Vatican where he made a profound impression
on the Pope, Clement VIII, who furnished him with letters
of introduction to various crowned heads of Europe. In
Portugal, he succeeded in re-converting a number of Marranos
to an open profession of Judaism, and one of them, a youth
named Diego Pires, who was actually serving as an official in
one of the state courts, threw up every honour and distinction,
assumed his ancestral Jewish name of Solomon Molcho and,
after a period as leader of the Kabbalists in Syria, came to
fulfil his own Messianic role in Rome. Here he sat in the

streets with the poor and outcast, and the story goes that, in an audience with the Pope, he prophesied that the eternal city would be devastated by a flood, an event which actually took place soon after, on 8 October 1530. But, like all the other messianic claimants, he came to a bad end. Though the Pope protected him from the Inquisition, he was finally burnt at the stake in Mantua (1532), a fate similar to that which ultimately befell his master Reubeni in Portugal. Although many of these pseudo-Messiahs lived partly by their wits, it would be incorrect to dismiss them as deliberate impostors. Within most of them was a mixture of fanatical belief and self-delusion.

Of special interest to English readers is the strange, romantic figure of an earlier 'messiah', David Alroy, who became the hero of an (unhistorical) novel by Benjamin Disraeli. He was a Persian Jew, educated in Baghdad, and after completing his studies he led an insurrection of his fellow-Jews against their Moslem rulers. He was proclaimed Messiah and was active around 1135-40 (or some say 1160). He was treacherously murdered by his own father-in-law, but for a long period after his death a Jewish sect called Menahemites ('consolers') held him in reverence as a man of surpassing beauty, courage and supernatural power.

Shabbetai Tzevi

The climax of this pseudo-Messianic development came with the rise and fall of the most remarkable of all these strange romantic figures, namely Shabbetai Tzevi. He was born in Smyrna in 1626 and his father was the Sephardi agent of an English merchant. He was profoundly influenced by the Kabbalistic School and indulged in all sorts of ascetic practices, mortifying his body with flagellation and bathing in the sea in the depths of winter. He had immense personal fascination and, when he became convinced that he was the long-awaited Messiah, the belief spread like wild-fire throughout the Jewish communities and even in some sectors of the Christian world.

According to biblical prophecy, the coming of the Messiah was to be heralded by the reappearance on earth of the prophet Elijah — that is why a special cup, called the cup of

Elijah, is still placed on the table of every Jewish home at the Passover Eve celebration: an unoccupied place, waiting to be filled, and kept empty against the coming of the Prophet. Shabbetai found his 'Elijah' in the person of a certain Nathan of Gaza who was prepared to serve his cause as the reborn prophet. He was fortunate, too, in the woman who became his wife: she, having lost her parents in a Polish massacre and been forcibly baptized, escaped from her convent firmly convinced that she was to marry the Messiah.

Although he had secretly announced himself to his followers as the Messiah in 1648, it was not until 1665 that Shabbetai took the crucial step of proclaiming himself openly as the 'Lord's Anointed' in the synagogue at Smyrna, and he immediately proceeded to divide the country of Palestine into provinces which he assigned to his devoted followers. Repercussions ensued all over the world. He ordained that the Fast of Av (the fifth month in the Jewish calendar), which had hitherto been a day of mourning and fasting in memory of the destruction of the Temple, was to be a feast day in honour of his birthday, with prayers offered up in all the synagogues for 'the holy, righteous, Shabbetai Tzevi, anointed of the God of Israel'.

At first, as might well have been expected, there was adverse rabbinic reaction to this new charlatanism, and the rabbinic authorities of Smyrna placed him under a ban. Later, Jacob Sasportas, the first rabbi of the Spanish and Portuguese Synagogue in London, who had moved to Amsterdam owing to the Great Plague, openly denounced him as an adventurous impostor. But the astonishing thing is that so little in the way of protest was aroused. The Jewish people as a whole seemed to have been seized with a wild hysteria. As he travelled from place to place, Shabbetai was everywhere acclaimed in an ecstasy of enthusiasm. Sober business men and many Spanish Marranos prepared to give up their occupations and depart for Palestine. The English Diarist, Samuel Pepys, writes of 'a Jew in town, that in the name of the rest do offer to give any man £10, to be paid £100 if a certain person now at Smyrna be within these two years owned by all the Princes of the East, and particular the Grand Segnor, as the King of the world'.

Yet in the end, as in the case of the other pseudo-Messiahs, Shabbetai's pretensions were unmasked and he was exposed as the charlatan he was. As a result of the opposition of the Smyrna rabbis, Tzevi had left for Salonika where he had kept the Jewish communities in Turkey in a state of ferment. Something like a political revolt seemed to be in the offing, and Shabbetai was therefore put in prison. Even there the mystique surrounding him continued unabated — vicarious suffering being part of the messianic role — and thousands of his admirers were allowed to enter the prison in order to pay him homage. A piece of contemporary doggerel written by a Christian runs as follows:

> And so in chains the Jews' redeemer lies,
> Yet in his presence are they in paradise;
> Humbly prostrate, and with reverence,
> They see, and do not see his impotence.

Then suddenly the Sultan intervened, warned, it is said, by a rival 'Messiah' from Poland, and Shabbetai was offered the alternative of death or apostasy. He chose the latter and he and many of his followers became converted to Islam.

This was not the end of the great illusion created by one of the most remarkable impostors in history. Many simple Jews still regarded him as the Jewish Messiah, believing his declaration that God himself had commanded him to accept the outward guise of another religion. Even after he died, a lonely outcast in Albania, the cult still survived, and learned rabbis continued to dispute about him and his claims in the communities of Poland and Germany. There is actually a Turkish sect today called the Donmeh ('apostates') who, outwardly Moslem, pray for the return of Shabbetai Tzevi, God's anointed messenger. Such were the persistent repercussions of the Kabbalist movement, and it is not surprising that the cult was finally excommunicated by the rabbis and the study of the *Zohar* prohibited.

10

JEWISH INFLUENCE ON THE
RENAISSANCE AND REFORMATION

The Jews of Florence

Though the word ghetto comes from Italy and shows
the kind of restrictions imposed on Italian Jews, yet,
by a curious paradox, the Jewish communities were on
the whole better treated there during the Middle Ages
than in any other European country. The reason for this
was probably twofold. Firstly, the general standard of
culture was higher among the Italian people than elsewhere, and they were therefore more inclined to appreciate
a cultured minority group like the Jews living in their
midst. Secondly, while the popes encouraged intolerance
towards the Jews in other Christian countries, they found
it expedient to make use of their financial and medical
skill nearer home. Certainly, whatever the reason, Italian
Jews, particularly in Florence, played a considerable part
in the general literary and humanistic development which
had its roots in Italy and later came to be known as the
Renaissance.

Even earlier than this a number of Italian Jews had identified themselves with the humanistic culture of the country
and produced literature which was reminiscent of that of the
ancient Greeks and somewhat alien to traditional Hebraic
and rabbinic thought. One such was Kalonymus (1286 - after
1328) who had settled in Rome and secured the patronage of
King Robert of Naples. Though primarily a scholar who
translated Arabic works of philosophy, mathematics, and
medicine into Hebrew and thence into Latin, he is chiefly
known as a satirist who had the audacity to write and circulate
a parody of the Talmud. Here is an extract from his book,
Touchstone, dealing with 'The Burden of Jewish Observance
on a Male':

> Its many laws and regulations,
> Which are unknown to other nations,

Every Hebrew must observe
With watchful eye and straining nerve,
E'en though he shares in public functions
He still must follow their injunctions,
Which I would tell you have been seen
To be six hundred and thirteen.

Another writer was Immanuel di Roma (*c.* 1265-1328) who produced a commentary on the Bible and, in his anxiety to identify general with Hebraic culture, maintained that all science was Jewish in origin. But he was above all a poet, who became the friend of Dante and took Boccaccio as his model. His verse has a typically frivolous touch:

Two Maids

Tamar, would I were a flower, tender and sweet,
To be trampled to earth by her pretty feet.
      Beriah, 'tis from fear of beholding her face
      That Messiah delayeth in showing his grace.
Tamar is enchanting, delighting the eyes,
Beriah a nightmare in woman's disguise.

Another poem is but a parody of Dante's *Inferno*, a typical passage running as follows:

At times in my spirit I fitfully ponder,
      Where shall I pass after death from this light,
Do heaven's bright glories await me, I wonder,
      Or Lucifer's kingdom of darkness and night?
In the one, though 'tis perhaps of ill reputation,
      A crowd of gay damsels will sit by my side;
But in heaven there's boredom and mental starvation.
      To hoary old men and to crones I'll be tied.

Later, in 1437, at the beginning of what may be called the Medici period, the Jewish community became established in Florence. Jews flourished under the Medici patrons of art and literature and were involved in that great awakening, the Renaissance, which spread through Europe and owed some of its early impetus to Jewish scholarship. Jewish translations of ancient Greek literature became widely known, first in Italy and then in other European countries, and gave the stimulus to a freedom of thought and imagination which characterized the revival of art and letters. Some members of the Jewish community belonged to the brilliant literary circle of Lorenzo the Magnificent, one in particular, Elijah del Medigo, becoming the greatest contemporary authority on Aristotle. Del Medigo studied at Padua — medicine, philosophy, mathematics and, under Galileo, astronomy. Settling in Florence, he exerted an indirect influence on Christian doctrine, for one of his Christian pupils, Pico de Mirandola, learnt from him the abstruse methods of deduction used by the Kabbalists and sought to prove the doctrine of the Trinity through numerical and alphabetical identification.

Abravanel

Another Jewish friend of Mirandola's, and an active participant in the Renaissance movement, was Judah Abravanel (c. 1460-c. 1521). The son of the famous Isaac Abravanel (see p. 83), he and his family were caught up in the Spanish Inquisition and fled to Naples and, subsequently, to Venice and Rome. He belonged to the most cultured Italian society, and his *Dialogues on Love* exerted a great influence on the philosophy and lyric poetry of the Renaissance period.

But this impact of Judaism and Jewish writers on the Renaissance was not a one-way traffic. The new enlightenment and freedom of thought which were implicit in its whole outlook had a deep effect on at least one famous Jewish book of the period, *The Enlightenment of the Eyes* (*Meor Enayim*) by Azariah di Rossi. It was this book, with its scientific approach to Jewish learning, that reintroduced after an interval of centuries the Apocryphal and Hellenistic writings, such as those of Philo and Josephus, to the Jewish reader. Rossi's researches were infused with the new, critical spirit of Italian humanism, but he did not sufficiently question his sources and frequently followed inaccurate records. His work, though highly valued by Hebraists, provoked opposition, as we have seen, in some rabbinic quarters.

Hebrew Printing

he invention of printing at this time had a marked effect in making Judaism better known both among its own devotees and to the adherents of other faiths. Again, Italy seems to have been the place where the first Jewish presses operated, though there is some evidence that as early as 1444 a German craftsman started printing from Hebrew manuscripts at Avignon (that is, before Gutenberg), and some fragments have recently come to light from pre-Expulsion days in Spain and Portugal. The first known printed book in Hebrew, however, was c. 1475, the product of a press set up at Reggio in the south of Italy.

Before the end of the fifteenth century 113 books had been printed in Hebrew and of these no less than 93 were Italian products. One family, called Soncino, played a conspicuous part in this process and was responsible for no less than a third of these publications, though their interest was by no means confined to the Hebraic and extended into the field of Latin and Italian literature as well. The Soncinos were named from a small town in Northern Italy, where in 1483 the physician, Israel Nathan Soncino, set up the printing-press with which the family is now mainly associated. A son and grandson carried on the work and the family moved to various Italian cities (Naples, Brescia, Rimini) and eventually — driven by competition — to Turkey. The excellence of their early Hebrew printing led to the founding in 1925 of the Soncino *Gesellschaft* in Berlin, as an association of Jewish bibliophiles, which produced annually several independent publications. After 1929, the name Soncino became known in England through the Soncino Press, which has published many specialized books of superb quality, including the thirty-four-volume Soncino Talmud.

Outside Italy, Jews were pioneers in printing in Portugal as well as on the continents of Africa and Asia, excluding China where the discovery probably anticipated that of Europe altogether. But the results of this new medium of literary dissemination were not wholly beneficial — comparable perhaps with the effects of television today. For one thing, since the majority of publications came from only one or two centres, such as Venice, this had a cramping effect on Jewish life and thought which tended to become stereotyped. For another, it became much easier for those hostile to the Jews to broadcast their slanders and at the same time impose a rigid censorship on all books emanating from Jewish sources.

Johannes von Reuchlin

Yet the invention of printing was an important factor in the spread of humanism and the revolt against rigid doctrinaire authority on the part of the Church or State, and there grew up within the Christian world at this period a new interest in Hebrew and post-biblical Judaism. This is well illustrated by the story of a great German scholar, Johannes von Reuchlin. His fame was to some extent due to a curious episode involving an unscrupulous Jewish convert called Pfefferkorn who, as so often happened, became the bitterest foe of his former religion and its adherents. In 1505, in order to ingratiate himself with his new co-religionists, Pfefferkorn became the voluntary agent of the Dominicans of Cologne who were determined to rid society of the newly printed Jewish literature as containing blasphemous, heretical teaching which sought to undermine the doctrines of the Church. At that time the largest Jewish community in Germany was in Frankfurt and, in carrying out the task with which he had been entrusted, Pfefferkorn sought and obtained from the Emperor Maximilian, in 1509, permission to destroy all the volumes of the Talmud and other Jewish literature in the possession of Frankfurt and Cologne Jews, as 'blaspheming' Christianity.

In this critical situation, it was the Christian Dominican, Reuchlin, who came to their rescue. This humanistic and genuinely religious man had studied Hebrew and Jewish literature under the tutorship of Jewish scholars in Italy and had become deeply impressed with Kabbalistic interpretations. When the leading Jews of Germany made their protest at the imperial court against the burning of their sacred and scholarly books, the Emperor Maximilian — and this showed the tremendous change which was coming over Europe as the result of the humanist movement — decided to consult an independent authority as to whether the Talmud and other

Jewish writings were actually hostile to Christianity. Reuchlin was an obvious choice. He pleaded eloquently against the destruction of Jewish books on the ground that they were in no way antagonistic to Christianity and suggested that they should be read rather than burnt. This led to a violent controversy between Reuchlin and his fellow Dominicans, in which Reuchlin, after receiving an adverse ruling from an ecclesiastical court, appealed to the Pope in Rome. Pope Leo X gave a formal verdict against Reuchlin, but the ban on Jewish books was not renewed. This conflict, in which the Dominicans were ranged against Reuchlin and the humanists, proved to be the first skirmishes that ultimately paved the way for the Reformation.

Luther and the Jews

The actual occasion which initiated the new movement and gave substance and immediacy to the deep-seated revolution in thought which was taking place at that time was the nailing by Martin Luther of a violent protest against the corruption of the Catholic establishment on his church door at Wittenberg. This courageous and independent-minded priest had studied Hebrew under Reuchlin and was greatly influenced by reading Rashi's commentary on the Hebrew Bible. He had come to the conclusion that genuine Christianity rested on biblical authority and that a break with the Papacy was essential if it was to remain true to its spiritual foundations. Hence arose the Protestant movement, first in Germany and then in other European countries, expressed in a living 'protest' against the established Church and resting on the basis of holy scripture.

But the first 'protesters' had been the Jewish people and, as was to be expected, Luther, following the precedents of John Hus and Reuchlin, started by expressing his warmest sympathy and support for his Jewish contemporaries. He wrote an essay entitled *Jesus Was Born a Jew* in which he stated in the most forthright terms:

They [the Jews] are blood-relations of our Lord: and if it were proper to boast of flesh and blood, the Jews belong to

Christ more than we. . . Therefore it is my advice that we
treat them kindly. . . We must exercise not the law of the
Pope, but that of Christian love, and show them a friendly
spirit. . .

And of their persecution by Christendom, he stated with
admirable frankness:

I would rather have been a pig than a Christian; they
treated the Jews as if they were dogs, not men. The Jews
are the best blood on earth through whom alone the Holy
Spirit gave the Holy Scriptures to the world. My advice
is that we treat them kindly — not driving them by force,
prohibiting them from working amongst us and forcing
them to be usurers.

Yet it became clear in later years that these generous
statements had an ulterior motive. Luther's underlying purpose was, as with his fellow-Christians, to convert Jews to the
true faith — that is to the newly interpreted Protestant Christianity which he himself had initiated. When his challenge
found no response, he turned against them with the utmost
bitterness and revived many of the libellous assertions — such
as that they poisoned the wells and murdered Christian
children at Passover — which he himself had repudiated when
attacking the Catholic Church. He even incited his followers
to burn Jewish books and destroy their synagogues.

So by a besetting irony of fate the Jewish people, who
had in a sense been one of the main agents in bringing about
the Reformation by keeping the spirit of true, unfettered
learning alive, began to suffer almost as much from the new
dispensation as the old Protestant Countries started to impose
the same kind of restrictions on them as the Catholic, and in
some cases carried out Luther's injunction to expel them altogether. And this time the situation was aggravated by the
fact that the Catholic Church held them responsible for the
new Christian heresy so that, when the reaction of the
Counter-Reformation set in, Jews became the worst sufferers
in the attempts to reinforce Papal authority and tighten up
the regulations with regard to heresy. They were subjected to

all the old horrors and restrictions of ghetto life, and this time there were no Reuchlins to espouse their cause.

Manasseh ben Israel

One of the brighter spots during the sixteenth century in Europe, however, where Jews could breathe more freely and give open expression to their particular way of life, was the Netherlands. Earlier, when Holland was under Spanish rule, Jews had suffered, together with the new Protestant heretics, under the cruelties of the Inquisition. But in 1567 William of Orange, Governor of Holland, took up the cause of Holland against Spain and of Protestantism against Catholicism. He failed at that time to unite all the provinces, but by 1579 the seven Protestant United Provinces had declared their independence from Spanish domination.

A large number of Marrano Jews flocked to Holland from the Iberian peninsula, threw over their outward conformity with Christianity and reasserted their allegiance to the Jewish way of life. What proved to be of special contemporary significance was the close relation between the thinking and written work which emanated from the new Rabbinic Academy at Amsterdam and the general lines on which the whole Reformation movement was developing. Among its rabbis was a disciple of Kabbalistic mysticism, Manasseh ben Israel, who had been taken by his family from Portugal to Holland as a year-old baby in 1605. At the early age of eighteen, he became Rabbi of the Amsterdam Synagogue and his writings began to attract a number of Christian scholars, so that henceforward he represented Jewish learning in the Christian world. It was through his contact with some of his Christian correspondents that he began to think of obtaining permission for the return of his own co-religionists to England.

Manasseh became interested in this as the result of a letter from an English friend, John Durie, which induced him to write a pamphlet, similar to the one written in the first century A.D., called *Contra Apionem*, by the Jewish historian Josephus. Manasseh called his document *Vindiciae Judaeorum* and sought to defend Jews against the usual charges and

calumnies by which they were vilified. But the religious
climate in England was already open to the acceptance of
these ideas and the consequent plea that Jews should be readmitted.

The first practical steps in regard to a possible return were
taken by those Puritan sects whose combined influence had
caused the overthrow of the monarchy and the establishment
of the Commonwealth. Such were the Levellers and the New
Covenanters who believed that the millennium would only
come about when Jews were to be found living among all the
nations of the world. The Levellers, indeed, called themselves
metaphorically 'Jews' and their enemies Amalekites. Another
group, the Fifth Monarchy men, held, concurrently with the
Jewish Kabbalists — who had been much influenced by the
Zohar, written in the fourteenth century (see p. 95) — that the
Messianic age was, so to speak, only just round the corner.
Finally, Manasseh received the support of Joanna and Ebenezer
Cartwright, English Baptists living in Holland, who sent a
petition to General Fairfax in favour of Jewish readmission.

Readmission to England

Jews had been expelled from England by Edward I in 1290
(see p. 79), but a small number of Marrano families still remained in London, and it has been suggested that the character
of Shylock in Shakespeare's *Merchant of Venice* owes its
origin to an actual Jewish doctor said to have been attending
Queen Elizabeth. When Manasseh appealed to Oliver Cromwell
to authorize the legal return of Jews to this country he was
invited to London to present his case. The Protector, partly
on grounds of religious toleration, partly through commercial
motives based on the theory that Jewish traders would benefit
England in their trade rivalry with Spain, supported Manasseh's
plea and called a conference in Whitehall (1655) consisting of
lawyers, religious leaders and merchants.

This led to a great deal of wrangling, in the course of which
a Jewish return to England was strongly opposed, on both
religious and commercial grounds. No conclusion was reached
and the conference was dismissed, so that Manasseh ben Israel
left England a disappointed man and died soon afterwards

believing that his mission had failed.

Actually, he succeeded far better than he knew, and the whole story illustrates the curiously illogical and pragmatic way in which political change has come about in this country. One vital admission had been made by the lawyers: that there was no legal bar to Jews settling in England. They were never formally readmitted by Act of Parliament, but a famous case in the law courts about this time tacitly recognized their existence as British citizens. Accordingly, the few Marranos in England gradually threw off their disguise and a small trickle of fresh Jewish immigrants came to join them. Two beneficial results followed, paradoxically enough, from Manasseh's failure to secure a separate legal status for the Jews in England. One was that they were never forced to live in a ghetto as in other European countries. This meant that there was a certain amount of social mixing with their Christian neighbours from the start: the latter not only did business with them but could see their synagogues — the first was a rented house in Creechurch Lane where they worshipped from 1657 to 1701, in which latter year the existing and very beautiful Bevis Marks Synagogue was built. It is almost certain, too, that had there been a law passed by the Commonwealth, establishing them as a protected community, it would have been replaced by the Parliament of the Restoration.

11

GROWTH OF JEWISH INTELLECTUALISM

The Jews of Holland

In the long story of the wanderings of the Jewish people we have seen how the Netherlands, as the result of their break-away from Spain, became one of the centres of Jewish life and rabbinic teaching. There is a curious romance associated with the foundation of the Amsterdam community. It was said that in 1593 a beautiful Portuguese Jewess, Maria Nuñez, fleeing persecution on a Portuguese ship, was captured with her brother when the vessel was taken by the English. She was brought to this country, where Queen Elizabeth was so fascinated by her that she set the passengers at liberty and offered them permission to settle in England — even, it is suggested, driving with Maria to show her the sights of London. Settlement in England, however, even under such protection, meant the eventual watering down of their religion so that, according to an ancient record, 'leaving all the pomp of England for the sake of Judaism', Maria and her brother proceeded to Amsterdam. Here they helped to found a Sephardi Jewish community, Maria later marrying one of her fellow refugees. It was the magnificent Portuguese Synagogue in Amsterdam (founded later in 1675) which formed the pattern for the Bevis Marks Synagogue in London.

Whether or not the emergence of the new Jewish community in Amsterdam can be accurately ascribed to Maria Nunez, it can be traced roughly to the period of her romantic adventure. Henceforth, Jews from the Spanish peninsula began to settle in Holland in comparatively large numbers. They threw off their Marrano disguise and developed a positive and vigorous synagogue life. At first, this was informed by traditional rabbinic concepts with the contemporary emphasis on Kabbalah. But later, as scholars imbued with the new philosophic and rationalistic outlook of the post-Renaissance period began to join the community, this old-established rabbinism was challenged — both here and in

Italy — by a growth of vigorous intellectualism. The seeds planted in the Jewish mind by Maimonides and the other original thinkers of the great Spanish period now bore fresh fruit in the free Jewish communities of Protestant European countries.

Reaction against the Shulhan Arukh

This new intellectualism came face to face with the rigidity of long-established religious practice and belief: a conflict all the more acute in view of the influence of Joseph Caro's *Shulhan Arukh* — the 'final' codification of Judaism, accepted as authoritative by the Jewish people as a whole. Religious codification in every denomination has its dangers, since it makes a claim of divine authority and leaves no room for the free exercise of the intellect or for any adaptation to the needs of a changing outlook and environment. This danger was intensified in the sixteenth century, as has been shown above, by the invention of the printing press which enabled the *Shulhan Arukh* to gain a unique verbal authority.

The Jews of Amsterdam, especially, were dominated by a *Shulhan Arukh* conformity, and any deviation from the multitudinous enactments of its code was regarded in the same way as the Christian Church regarded heresy. Inevitably there was antagonism and, indeed, bitter controversy between those who held to a strictly authoritarian orthodoxy and those who followed the new intellectualism — fuelled, understandably, by the Marranos who were then experiencing freedom of thought after years of oppression and underground activity in Spain and Portugal.

Uriel Acosta

In such a situation it was inevitable — human nature being very much the same everywhere — that conflict should break out, and this is illustrated by the stories of two 'deviationists' who, tragically, received the harshest treatment at the hands of their establishment.

Uriel Acosta was born in Portugal about 1585, of Marrano descent from a family who had been, at least outwardly, Catholic for generations. As a young scholar, he secretly studied the scriptures and gradually there grew within him the craving to revert to the religion of his ancestors. He succeeded in converting his family, and they fled to Amsterdam so that they could openly practise their faith.

Unfortunately, the young student found a very different Judaism flourishing there from the one which had conquered his heart. His was the idealistic Judaism of the Prophets, not the formalism of the *Shulhan Arukh*. Like the Karaites (see p. 55), it' was the biblical religion rather than the rabbinic that he desired, and accordingly he wrote a book in which he attacked contemporary religious practices and passionately sought to persuade the Jews of Amsterdam to adopt his reformist views. But the time was not ripe for such a revolution in thought. It was understandable that those who had suffered persecution for centuries on account of their religion should wish to keep it intact and should look with suspicion on anyone who wished to tamper with its established form. Acosta was immediately excommunicated by the Synagogue and thrown into prison by the local authorities to whom the rabbis had appealed.

From prison he escaped to Germany, where he lived for nine years in complete isolation. Finally, longing to return to his family and Jewish communal life, he begged the Amsterdam community to forgive him and allow him to return. This they did, and for a time he lived peaceably among them. But such an accommodation, involving a total sacrifice of his sincerely held convictions, could not last. His intellectual and rationalistic outlook did not permit him to accept a supernaturally revealed religion, and reports began to reach the rabbis that he was neglecting the rites and ordinances of the rabbinic code.

This led to a second excommunication, and once again, this time for seven years, he suffered the mortification of one who was ostracized both by family and from communal life. Again, he made a public recantation of his views. This time the authorities insisted on an official act of penance which, ironically, had its roots in the Christian Inquisition. He was forced to make confession of his sins in a crowded synagogue, following which he was flogged. These humiliations were unendurable and he committed suicide immediately afterwards. Such was the tragic end of a deeply sensitive man who was temperamentally unable to stand up to opposition and permanent estrangement from his family and community.

Benedict de Spinoza (1632-77)

Uriel Acosta's independent, intellectual outlook exercised a profound influence on the greatest Jewish thinker of the day and one of the greatest philosophers of all time, Benedict de Spinoza. Born in Amsterdam in 1632, Spinoza was nurtured in the free cultural environment of his native city and as a youth studied not only the Talmud and the later Kabbalistic literature, but also Latin, science and philosophy. Among his teachers was the famous Manasseh ben Israel, primarily responsible for the return of Jews to England.

But it was above all the spirit of protest inherited from Acosta that he expressed in his life and outlook and which, more than anything else, shaped his destiny. He could not accept the fundamentalism inherent in Rabbinic Judaism and openly expressed heretical opinions about certain traditional beliefs (such as angels, heaven, and hell) which, he maintained, conflicted with reason. He went so far as to say that 'All religions are good that lead to a good life: you need not seek further'. In this he was merely echoing the old rabbinic saying that 'the righteous of all peoples shall inherit the Kingdom to come', but, in the age in which he lived, a reaction was setting in, as we have seen in the case of Acosta. The Jewish religious authorities, partly, it must in fairness be said, owing to their own increasing insecurity vis-à-vis the Dutch Government, determined to stamp out all forms of heresy within the community.

At the age of twenty-three, Spinoza was excommunicated. Unlike Acosta, he refused to recant and for the rest of his life he wandered about from village to village, finally settling at the Hague. He made many friends among its non-Jewish inhabitants and earned his livelihood as an optician — an occupation which led to his death at the age of forty-five, as the dust from the lenses he manufactured entered his lungs and gradually brought on a fatal consumptive illness.

It is one of the ironies of history that today the rabbis who drove Spinoza out of the Synagogue are unknown, while their victim is regarded as one of the two great founders of modern philosophy (the other being the French philosopher Descartes).

His aim was always the pursuit of the ideal life. 'I determined', he wrote, 'to search out whether there were not something truly good and communicable to man, by which his spirit might be affected to the exclusion of all other things: yea, whether there were anything, through the discovery and acquisition of which I might enjoy continuous and perfect gladness for ever.' In one of his works (*Tractatus Theologicus-Politicus*), he advocates freedom of conscience and the separation of religion from the state. 'What can be more fatal a step than to treat as enemies men who have committed no other crime than that of believing independently?' he wrote. In his greatest work, the *Ethics*, he developed his ideas of God and showed that he was opposed to the dualism of Aristotle and Descartes. He taught that each finite thing is in God and God is immanent in all things — which is the metaphysics of pantheism. Nature and God were one substance 'in whose negative abyss everything individual lies buried'. 'It is man's duty to merge that which is individual and perishable, that is, his passions and emotions, in the infinite substance which is God.' Though Orthodox Judaism rejected him on account of his refusal to believe in a personal God, subsequent generations called him the 'God-intoxicated' Jew. Here is a sample of his reasoning:

> This being so, we may with reason regard as a great absurdity what many, who are otherwise esteemed as great theologians, assert, namely, that if no eternal life resulted from the love of God, then they would seek what is best for themselves: as though they could discover anything better than God! This is just as silly as if a fish (for which, of course, it is impossible to live out of the water) were to say: if no eternal life is to follow this life in the water, then I will leave the water for the land.

It should not be thought, however, that the freedom of the Netherlands petered out in oppression, and that the only true contributors to Jewish thinking were persecuted rebels. Amsterdam produced a glittering array of Jewish scholars, artists, poets, and authors who, although they may not have attracted individually the attention given to the more colourful lives of Acosta and Spinoza, laid the foundations of a great Jewish community.

Outside the religious sphere, Jews were particularly influential in the art and technique of diamond-polishing, a craft which remained almost entirely in the hands of Jewish workers until the twentieth century. Throughout the nineteenth century, the Amsterdam Jewish community, with its well-organized institutions, its great libraries and its strong Jewish loyalties, remained one of the most important in the world. Amsterdam Jews suffered immeasurably during the mass deportations of the Nazis, their numbers dropping from 86,000 to about 14,000.

Italian Rationalists

Italy as well as Holland became a centre of Jewish intellectualism after the Spanish period, and many of the Marrano families settled there. Two Italian contemporaries of Spinoza deserve special mention as exemplifying the current tendency to give a rationalistic interpretation of Judaism: Joseph Solomon ben Elijah del Medigo, grandson of the Aristotelian scholar Elijah del Medigo (see p. 102) and Leone da Modena. The former, a brilliant but often insincere scholar, fearful of accusations of heresy, led a wandering life, oscillating in his opinions between Kabbalah and scientific knowledge. He was a pupil of Galileo and one of the first Hebrew writers to defend the astronomical discoveries of both Galileo and his forerunner, Copernicus.

Leone Modena, scholar, rabbi, and poet, was a versatile Italian Jew, one of whose main objects was to interpret Judaism to contemporary Christians — he wrote a handbook for the instruction of the English king, James I. At the age of fourteen he produced his 'Dialogue against Gambling' which passed through ten editions and was translated into Latin,

French, and German. Unfortunately, he displayed an in-
stability of character hardly compatible with his teaching,
and, ironically, became the leader of a gambling coterie in the
Venetian ghetto. Being too weak-willed to overcome it, he
attributed his failing to the astral influences under which he
had been born. Modena, however, was a brilliant preacher,
and his writings brought him in touch with leading non-Jewish
scholars to whom he represented Jewish scholarship.

In addition to his preaching and teaching (which attracted
large audiences, including Christian priests and noblemen) he
exercised no less than twenty-six professions (press-corrector,
notary, bookseller, director of the theatre and musical
academy etc.). His letters and autobiography (one of the
earliest in Hebrew) throw much light on the social conditions
of his day.

Jewish Drama

In spite of a certain austerity or what might be described as a
puritanical outlook in the traditional rabbinic mentality due
to a horror of anything savouring of idolatry, Jewish life at
this period was not without its aesthetic side. Drama, in
particular, has always appealed to Jews, and it is recorded
that, when Mantua became the centre of Italian drama, the
court performances had to be held especially early on a Friday
afternoon so that Jewish actors and members of the audience
could get to their homes in time to observe the inauguration
of the Sabbath. Moreover, although the rabbis tended to
frown on dramatic performances as well as dancing, they
seem to have made an exception in the case of the book of
Esther — which was turned into a play for the festival of
Purim — as well as a number of other biblical themes.

After the Renaissance period, Jews began to take part in
theatrical performances both as writers and actors with their
Christian friends, and the first treatise on dramatic art was
written by an Italian Jew. In Holland, too, during and after
the lifetime of Spinoza, plays of the 'morality' type, based on
the stories of the Old Testament, came to be written in many
languages, the earliest, called *Foundations of the World,* by
Moses Zacuto, being based on the story of Abraham.

Luzzatto

Side by side with the development of drama a fresh vitality
came to Hebrew poetry as a direct result of the Kabbalistic
or mystical movement previously described. This received its
fullest expression in the allegorical, dramatic poetry of Moses
Hayyim Luzzatto (1707-47). He was born in Padua, and his
poems showed him to be a man of exceptional genius though,
in earlier life, as so frequently happened with Kabbalists, his
mind was dominated by the extravagant fancies of mystical
thought. He gathered round him a circle of students of the
esoteric, practised mystical austerities, and believed himself
to be the Messiah. Rather naturally, he was opposed by the
Italian rabbis, who feared another Shabbetai Tzevi, and under
pressure he left Italy, settling eventually in Amsterdam where
he supported himself as a diamond polisher. In 1743, he
emigrated to Palestine and died of the plague at Acre.

Nevertheless, Luzzatto must be regarded as the true descendant of Judah Ha-Levi (see p. 64), and his inspired writings
marked the beginning of a new era, gaining for him the title
of 'the father of modern Hebrew'. His greatest work was
called *Praise to the Righteous* and expressed in poetic language
the perpetual struggle between truth and falsehood:

> Truly our eyes are deluded, for eyes of flesh they are.
> Therefore they change truth into falsehood, darkness they
> make light, and light darkness. An accident suffices to
> distort our view of tangible things; how much more do we
> stray from the truth with things beyond the reach of our
> senses. See the oars in the water. They seem crooked and
> twisted. Yet we know them to be straight.

The Later Theatre

The Hebrew theatre proper is a development of the twentieth
century, but from the eighteenth century onwards there were
outstanding Jewish actors in many European countries,
including Rachel and Sarah Bernhardt in nineteenth-century
France. One of the most famous of Jewish theatre companies
is the *Habimah,* founded in Moscow in 1918 and transplanted
about 1925 to Palestine.

The Yiddish theatre originated in the Middle Ages, with the Purim plays, and long remained very much in the style of the mediaeval mystery plays on biblical subjects. Later, in the nineteenth century, Yiddish players followed the waves of Jewish immigrants to the United States, and the Yiddish theatre broadened into original as well as translated plays and musicals, one of the best-known Yiddish dramatists being the American poet H. Leivick (the pseudonym of Leivick Halper), author of *The Golem*.

The Hebrew theatre is indeed a very ancient, though not by any means continuous, institution. It is believed to go back to early times. The Song of Miriam (Exod. 15.20 f.) and the Song of Solomon, as well as Job, are considered by many to be dramatic in form and intention.

12

HASIDIC MOVEMENT IN EASTERN EUROPE

Revolt against Rabbinic Austerity

One of the most fascinating features of Jewish history is the way in which it is inextricably bound up with the development of the nations among whom the Jewish people lived. This is nowhere better illustrated than in the case of Poland. We have seen that many Jews found refuge there (see ch. 8) during the period of the Inquisition and that, comparatively speaking, they were tolerantly treated. They rendered, in fact, a valuable service to the national economy, for they became stewards on the estates of the Catholic nobles, rent-collectors for the land-owners, travelling merchants, and even innkeepers in many of the villages. This apparent security led to so large an influx that there were probably more Jews in Poland during this period than in all the other countries put together.

But Polish history has been dominated by violence and conquest. In 1648, the local Cossacks — Russian peasants who, it must be remembered, belonged to the Greek Orthodox Church and were kept in penury and subjection in order to do the spade-work on the farms and estates — rose in revolt against their Catholic overlords. This proved to be disastrous for the Jewish estate-agents and rent-collectors who, as 'go-betweens', exacting the overlords' exorbitant rents and taxes, were the immediately visible and unlucky objects of resentment — even more hated than their masters. When the Cossack rebellion broke out in 1648, under a ruthless leader called Chmielnicki, one of the worst massacres in Jewish history took place, in which whole communities were pitilessly destroyed.

Later, the Russians, who regarded the Cossacks as their subjects, invaded Poland and vented their animosity not only on the Polish Catholics who ruled over them but also on the Jews, who had identified with their Polish masters. Indeed, the latter capitalized on the unpopularity of their Jewish agents and, right through the period of conquest carried out by both Russians and Swedes (1605-58), they managed to escape some of the worst atrocities by using Jews as their scapegoats. Thus Jewish massacres of the most appalling intensity took place, and those who survived were ultimately banished from the new Cossack settlements. Poland, indeed, as a country and quite apart from its Jewish inhabitants, has always been the unhappy scene of national aggression and conquest, and the Jewish factor only serves to emphasize the point already made that Jewish history is inextricably linked with the history of the European nations of which they formed a part.

Possibly as the result of this continuous harassment and suffering, it was in Poland that a new Jewish religious movement now emerged. Once again there was a break-away from the old rabbinic austerity and scholasticism which had failed to satisfy the emotional needs of the humble, suffering masses. The persecuted poor craved for consolation and joy, something which would appeal to their hearts and enable them to escape from the rigours of their daily lives. The new sect which supplied this need were called *Hasidim* ('righteous'), a term borrowed from a similar Jewish group in early days (see p. 26). Gone, in their case, was the dry intellectualism of the north, and an almost frenzied emotionalism took its place.

Baal Shem Tov

The new movement of Hasidism received its life and impetus from one of the most remarkable figures in Jewish history. About the year 1700, there was born in one of the southern Polish provinces, Podolia, a child named Israel ben Eliezer who soon showed certain unusual qualities that marked him out from his contemporaries. He hated school (like many other boys right up to modern times, including Winston Churchill), played truant from time to time when he should have been at his *Heder*, and wandered off alone into the woods and fields of his countryside. He was finally expelled and, from the age of twelve, was compelled to earn his own living, first as a helper in the school, then as *Shammash* (sexton) in the synagogue, where he often spent whole nights in prayer. Later, when adult, he became a lime-burner in his local Podolian village, and after that a slaughterer.

It was during his youthful wanderings through country and village, in close contact with nature and simple human beings, that he developed the mystical approach to truth which subsequently dominated his whole thought and action. It was not, however, the mysticism of the earlier Kabbalists with its element of austerity and self-mortification that appealed to him, but that of intense humanism and the kind of ecstatic joy that took heaven by storm. To him, as to Elizabeth Barrett Browning, 'Earth's crammed with heaven, and every common bush afire with God'. Religion, in his view, was a matter of feeling and emotion, rather than of learning, and he had little use for the scholastic methods of the old Talmudic school of thought. In particular, he broke away from tradition in his attitude to the simpleton, the peasant, the *Am ha-aretz* so much despised by the traditional rabbinic scholar who held that learning was a test of religion and 'that no ignoramus could be a pious person'.

He went about like his great Jewish predecessor, Jesus of Nazareth, bringing comfort and healing to the ailing, the mentally sick, and the poverty-stricken through the medium of emotional fervour and ecstatic prayer. He gained a large following among the peasant folk, who flocked to him for advice and help when they were in distress and even came to regard him as something of a miracle-worker. It was through this capacity to minister to the needs of simple folk that he won the title, by which he is known to history, of Baal Shem Tov: 'Master of the Good Name' (of God).

A Religion of Joy

The followers of this movement, who, as we have seen, came to be called Hasidim after the pious resisters to secular authority at the time of the Hasmoneans, infused a spirit of merriment and light-heartedness into their religion for the first time in Jewish history, and it spread like wildfire through Poland, Hungary and Rumania. For a time, indeed, it became a serious threat to the more austere Talmudic

Judaism since its rapturous quality appealed to the ordinary, unthinking man in the street. At its best it was intensely human and emphasized the loving, compassionate, deeply sympathetic aspects of Jewish teaching. Here are some Hasidic stories:

> A father complained to the Baal Shem that his son had forsaken God. 'What, Rabbi, shall I do?' 'Love him more than ever,' was the Baal Shem's reply.

> A Rabbi ordered his Warden to assemble ten men for a *Minyan* (quorum) to chant Psalms for the recovery of a sick man. When they entered, a friend of the Rabbi exclaimed: 'I see among them notorious thieves.' 'Excellent,' retorted the Rabbi. 'When all the Heavenly Gates of Mercy are closed, it requires experts to open them.'

> To sin against a fellow-man is worse than to sin against the Creator. The man you harmed may have gone to an unknown place, and you may lose the opportunity to beg his forgiveness. The Lord, however, is everywhere and you can always find Him when you seek Him.

> A little farmer boy, having been left an orphan at an early age, was unable to read, but had inherited a large, heavy prayer book from his parents. On the Day of Atonement he brought it into the synagogue, laid it on the reading desk, and, weeping, cried out: 'Lord of Creation! I do not know how to pray; I do not know what to say — I give Thee the entire prayer book.'

> Rabbi Moshe Leib of Sasov once gave his last coin to a man of evil reputation. His students reproached him for it. Whereupon he replied: 'Shall I be more particular than God, who gave the coin to me?'

The Tzaddik

But there was another less reputable development from Hasidism which departed almost totally from the spirit which had animated the Baal Shem and his immediate followers. This consisted of the kind of miracle-mongering and mystic mumbo-jumbo which have so often bedevilled religious revivalist movements in the history of almost every faith. Even in the Baal Shem's own community there had been the belief that a few men, called the Tzaddikim or Righteous, were endowed with exceptional spiritual gifts and insights which enabled them to approach more closely to God than the average and to commune directly with him.

This belief degenerated after the Baal Shem's death into a widespread superstition of the crudest kind, as a result of which a few of these wonder-workers received an almost slavish worship from their ignorant and credulous followers. Gifts were showered upon them, as, in the days of paganism, idolators bribed their idols, hoping to receive thereby all sorts of material benefits including miraculous cures from disease. This, as can be imagined, led to many abuses on the part of the Tzaddik rabbis, some of whom became unscrupulous charlatans, taking advantage of the simplicity of the masses to gain power and wealth for themselves and building up something resembling the splendid courts of a Polish prince. Drinking and wild dancing characterized the religious festivals of the movement, and in time the office of Tzaddik even became invested with hereditary rights in the minds of its supporters, who thought that the son of an original Tzaddik had inherited the miraculous gifts of his father.

Decline of Hasidism

Inevitably such movements, resting as they did on an appeal to emotionalism, sensuality, and superstition provoked opposition from the traditional scholarly Rabbinate, and a counter-movement started when a secret anti-Hasidic meeting-place was founded at Vilna in 1772. This was led by the local Gaon, Elijah ben Solomon (1720-97) who has been called 'the last of the rabbinical giants of the heroic age'. His supporters became known as Mitnaggedim (opponents) and they decreed a ban against the Hasidim and attempted to excommunicate them from the Jewish fold.

This led to something approaching a schism in east European Jewry, and it looked as though the community might permanently be split in two. But fortunately, owing largely

to the rabbinic gift for compromise and the warm humanity
for their opponents, the better elements in Hasidism came to
be recognized as being within the spirit and ethos of traditional Judaism. This tolerance on the part of the Mitnaggedim evoked a corresponding gesture from the Hasidim who
henceforth acknowledged the learning and piety of the
rabbis. Thus their movement was prevented from becoming a
schismatic one and, though its influence gradually declined,
there remains a Hasidic element in the Jewish community
right up to the present day. Indeed, in recent years many
reputable Jewish writers — not least Martin Buber, the great
scholar, Zionist and religious philosopher, whose death
occurred only a few years ago — have sought to interpret
what was best in Hasidic thought and practice for the benefit
of contemporary religious thinkers.

13

ERA OF EMANCIPATION

Dawn of Tolerance
One of the biggest issues facing mankind today is that raised
by the emergence of a multi-cultural, multi-racial society.
Even now we have not learnt to accept the principle of unity
in diversity, and much of the social disharmony and bitterness which characterizes the modern scene arises from man's
inability to accept differences, particularly of race, religion
and colour.

The modern concept of tolerance had its roots in the new
ideas about the rights of man which began to spread over
Europe in the second half of the eighteenth century.
Advanced thinkers, such as John Locke in our own country
and Voltaire in France, started an intellectual process concerned with the principle of freedom and human equality, and
it was the Jews, hitherto regarded as the outcasts of society,
who benefited most from this Age of Enlightenment.

In this context, it is interesting to note that the first
European to set foot on the continent of America (actually
discovered in the year of the Jewish expulsion from Spain,
1492) was probably a Marrano Jew, Luis de Torres, who went
as interpreter to Columbus's first expedition. There is no
doubt, too, that Christopher Columbus was greatly encouraged in his projected exploration across the Atlantic by
geographers, astronomers and mathematicians such as Diego
de Deza and Abraham Zacuto, who were either Jewish or of
Jewish descent. In particular, Zacuto (*c.* 1450-1515) was an
astronomer and historian of great distinction. He was the first
to make a metal astrolabe, and he drew up improved astronomical tables which were invaluable as guides to navigation.
These were used by Columbus, and a copy is preserved in
Seville bearing the explorer's own annotation. When the Jews
were expelled from Spain, Zacuto became court astronomer to
King John II of Portugal, where he was consulted by Vasco da

Gama before the latter sailed to India in 1497. Shortly after this, Jews were expelled from Portugal, and Zacuto, after many wanderings, settled in Tunis.

The first European monarch to pass an 'Edict of Toleration' was Joseph II of Austria. This was in 1782 and, by abolishing the Jewish badge and poll tax (a special tax, by payment of which Jews were permitted to live in Austria, though not protected), it effectively started the process whereby Jews were ultimately recognized as human beings with the same rights as other citizens of the countries to which they belonged. In 1791, with the cry of '*Liberté, Égalité, Fraternité*' and the Revolution that followed, France abolished all anti-Jewish laws. Holland followed suit in 1796, and even Prussia, the most chauvinistic of all European states, began to grant civil rights to its Jewish citizens in 1812. In England, with its typical propensity for letting things drift — on the principle of '*solvitur ambulando*' — full political rights were not secured till much later, but the social integration of Jews had already begun and they never suffered any persecution here after the Resettlement in 1656.

Moses Mendelssohn
This era of European enlightenment and emancipation threw up one figure who dominated both the Jewish and general intellectual scene of the time, and the influence of his writings and personality has profoundly affected the whole subsequent history of Judaism. He was born in the year 1729 at Dessau into one of the famous German-Jewish families, his name being originally Moses son of Mendel, which afterwards took its German form. As a little, hunchbacked but sweet-tempered boy he used to be carried by his father, a poor Torah-scribe, to the local rabbinic school where he studied with unquenchable enthusiasm under Rabbi David Fränkel. When the latter was appointed Chief Rabbi of Berlin, his pupil, contrary to the wishes of his parents who wanted him to take up a trade, trudged off after him and arrived at the Berlin 'Jews' gate, footsore and weary, five days after his departure.

In those days — we might compare the wall dividing Berlin today — it was not easy for a poor boy tramp to get through, but he was finally admitted. Touched, no doubt, by the boy's religious ardour and passionate determination to continue studying under him, Rabbi Fränkel immediately tackled the problem of his extreme poverty, allowed him to sleep in an attic in his house, gave him dinner on Sabbaths and Festivals and arranged for a friend to supplement the meals he was able to earn for himself.

By dint of hard study, Mendelssohn managed not only to deepen his rabbinic knowledge but to acquire a mastery of the German language and a working knowledge of Latin, French, English and, later, Greek. He also studied mathematics and philosophy, and his wonderful command of German enabled him in 1763 to win the Berlin Academy of Sciences Prize with his essay on metaphysics, defeating, among others, the great German philosopher, Immanuel Kant. Such achievements resulted both in financial security, after years of semi-starvation, and acceptance at the highest cultural and scientific levels of the time. He became a partner in a silk-mercer's firm where he had once been a clerk, and obtained entry into a prominent literary circle which used to meet in a coffee-house for the purpose of playing chess and discussing current political and philosophical problems.

It was here that he met the great German poet Lessing, and the two became close friends. One result of their intimacy was the writing of a play which had a profound bearing not only on the contemporary German scene but on subsequent generations throughout Europe. This was Lessing's *Nathan der Weise*, the chief character of which was a thinly veiled portrait of Mendelssohn himself. The setting was Jerusalem at the time of Saladin, and the play's unique and revolutionary quality consisted in the presentation of nobility on the part of the Jewish and Moslem characters and cruel intolerance in the person of the Christian Patriarch.

It was through his metaphysical works that Mendelssohn gradually rose to fame and was accepted, in spite of being a Jew, as a leading German philosopher (in fact, Frederick the Great conferred on him the status of 'Protected, or Court Jew', and this freed him from most of the contemporary Jewish disabilities). His most famous work the *Phädon* (based

on Plato's dialogue the *Phaedo*) was an attempt to con-
vince a sceptical age that man's soul is immortal. Its chief
arguments, rooted in an acceptance of the existence of God,
were as follows:

a　　If the body (matter) does not perish, but passes into
other forms, surely the soul that dominates the body is
imperishable.

b　　We find this belief in immortality implanted in our
being and we cannot conceive that God would deceive his
children by imbuing them with a false hope.

c　　Life is a charge, not an absolute possession; therefore
man has no right to extinguish it.

Mendelssohn's influence on subsequent Jewish life in the
Diaspora can hardly be exaggerated. He translated the Pentateuch into German written in Hebrew characters, and added a
Hebrew commentary which broke away to some extent from
that of the rabbis. This was a means of introducing the Jews to
German literature and culture, and raising them out of the rut
of the ghetto. At the same time, he presented Judaism to
them in a form which did not conflict with the cultural and
scientific climate of the age, and made it possible for Jews to
be fully Germanic and yet remain faithful to their religion. In
his *Jerusalem*, he wrote: 'Comply with the customs and the
civil constitutions of the countries in which you are transplanted, but, at the same time, be constant to the faith of
your forefathers.' Here we have a late echo of Jeremiah's
wonderful injunction to his fellow-Jews who were being
forcibly transplanted to distant Babylon, which has remained
a permanent appeal to Diaspora Jews to observe the principle
of good citizenship: 'And seek the peace of the city whither I
have caused you to be carried away captive, and pray unto the
Lord for it: for in the peace thereof shall ye have peace.'

Yet the movement started by Mendelssohn for cultural
assimilation on the part of the Jewish community was not
without its dangers, at least from the Jewish religious point of
view. For it meant, in the case of many Jews, a weakening of
the ties which bound them to their ancestral faith and a
willingness to compromise in matters of belief and practice.

Thus many of his followers (including his own family and his grandson, the composer) left their faith and became converts to Christianity. One not altogether surprising result of the popularity of his literary works among Christians was an attempt on the part of a Swiss clergyman, Lavater, to convert Mendelssohn himself to Christianity. Lavater, in his admiration for the Jewish philosopher, actually dedicated one of his works, *Proofs of Christianity*, to him and invited him to join in a public discussion on the relative merits of the two faiths. Mendelssohn's reply was as follows: 'Of the essentials of my Faith I am so indisputably assured that I shall ever adhere to it. The doctrines of the despised Judaism are more consistent with reason than those of Christianity. For it consists of "natural religion" supplemented by certain statutes.' Lavater, to his credit, offered Mendelssohn a sincere apology.

In spite of the risks he ran in the struggle for emancipation, Judaism and the Jewish people owe an eternal debt to Mendelssohn, for *Haskalah* (enlightenment) has remained ever since an integral part of the whole Jewish religious outlook. He showed that there was nothing incompatible in the observance of a distinctive faith and complete identification with enlightened secular patterns of thought. Partly by his metaphysical thinking derived from Greek philosophy — he was a 'new Socrates' both in mind and appearance — partly through his translations of the Pentateuch and Psalms in the German vernacular, he developed a new image in the Jewish mind of the Jew as 'a German of the Jewish faith', which combined loyalty both to his country and his religion. And this has been the model ever since for Jews living widely scattered in the various countries of the world.

French Revolution and Paris Sanhedrin
In spite of this cultural or intellectual enlightenment (the Haskalah movement, as it is called) for which Moses Mendelssohn was largely responsible, it must not be thought that the Jewish communities in Europe had secured, by the time of his death in 1786, anything like political emancipation or full civil rights. It was to be a long uphill struggle before

this final stage was reached, but by one of the curious coincidences of history — again it would be a hazardous guess whether this was *post hoc* or *propter hoc* — there occurred shortly afterwards a violent national upheaval which had the most far-reaching consequences for Jews all over Europe, namely the French Revolution. This came about as the result of an egalitarian movement fostered by such writers as Voltaire, Rousseau, and Diderot, and it took practical shape when the French mobs rose in revolt against the monarchy and aristocratic government.

In 1784 King Louis XVI was forced to summon a 'National Assembly', whose function it was to implement the principle of human rights. Naturally, in the declaration that followed, the rights of Jewish citizens could not be ignored, and a decree passed by the assembly in 1791 finally abolished all Jewish disabilities. Thus, though the principle had been established a few years earlier in the newly formed United States of America, France was the first European country to accord full civil rights to its Jewish minority.

There followed the reign of terror centred in Paris when the king, queen, and the much-hated aristocrats were guillotined by the French mob. A few individual Jews, owing to their identification with the aristocracy, suffered a similar fate. Further, with the enthronement of the goddess of Reason, all religious institutions including the Synagogue were closed and an experiment was tried of resting every tenth instead of every seventh day, thus abolishing both Sabbath and Sunday observances.

This chaotic situation was brought under some measure of control by the meteoric rise of the young Corsican general, Napoleon Buonaparte. He gave direction to the movement through a long campaign of foreign conquest and, wherever the Revolutionary armies penetrated, they established the principle of equality, which incidentally included Jewish emancipation. In Holland, when Jews gained full citizenship in 1796, they almost immediately secured the right to be elected members of the legislative council. In Venice the Italians burned down the ghetto gates, and henceforth Jews could take part in Italian municipal government and obtain commissions in the National Guard.

The most sensational result of Napoleon's conquests from the Jewish point of view came about as the result of certain ideas he conceived during his Egyptian campaign. It was there that he became absorbed with the old romantic dream of a Jewish return to the Holy Land, and he proposed to the Jewish communities of the Middle East that they should support the French army in an attempt to deliver Jerusalem from Turkish rule. After his victory at Austerlitz (1805), however, he seems to have had second thoughts which led him to form, instead, a Jewish Council consisting of 150 Jewish notables which subsequently (in 1807) he turned into a new Sanhedrin (see p. 40). In conformity with the ancient pattern this Sanhedrin was composed of seventy-one members, two-thirds being rabbis and the rest laymen. In response to questions about the attitude of Judaism to the French State, the Sanhedrin then adopted the following regulations:

1. The non-Israelitish monotheist was to be regarded as a brother.
2. Jews must defend and serve their country.
3. Agriculture and handicrafts were to be encouraged, as demanded by Jewish law.
4. The practice of usury was to be forbidden.
5. Monogamy was to be the only recognized form of marriage.
6. Intermarriage was to be treated as binding, though not to be accompanied 'by a Jewish ceremony'.
7. A civil marriage must precede the religious.
8. A Jewish divorce must be preceded by a civil decree.

The Sanhedrin regulated the pattern of Jewish life throughout the French Empire until Napoleon's final defeat at Waterloo. As can be seen from these resolutions, the pattern was strongly assimilationist in character and, therefore, a mixed blessing from the standpoint of distinctive Jewish faith. Nevertheless it captured Jewish imagination and very largely secured their support for the Emperor.

Ghetto Walls Fall

The Napoleonic victories, then, brought about in the political sphere what Mendelssohn's literary work had achieved in the cultural, namely the breaking down of the ghetto. This had incalculable effects on Jewish social and religious development, for Jews now found themselves an integral part of their national communities to an extent that had not obtained since the Golden Age in Spain. It is true that social discrimination still remained, for people cannot be made tolerant through legislation, especially when prejudices are deeply entrenched and have the centuries-old sanction of officialdom and public opinion behind them. Yet it was impossible for Jews ever to return in spirit to ghetto life after they had tasted the fruits of freedom and equality.

There was, however, a serious reaction in many countries after Napoleon's downfall, due partly to the general revulsion against a foreign dictatorship. The Treaty of Vienna, in spite of the liberal views expressed by some of the national delegates, only secured for Jews those rights which they had held before the French conquests. Germany proved to be the most reactionary of the powers, and something like the old ghetto was restored to Frankfurt. In Prussia, Jews were disfranchized and in some towns even attacked and exiled. Papal authority was re-established in Italy with all its anti-Jewish restrictions, and in some parts of Europe the number of Jewish marriages was limited by law and Jewish children were even forbidden non-Jewish forenames.

Yet these legalistic attempts to put the clock back and restore the old status of inferiority for the Jewish minorities in Europe failed on the whole to achieve their purpose. The process of emancipation had gone too far, either for Jews to accept the old role of humiliation or for their gentile neighbours to conceive of them any longer in terms of an alien, inferior group. Familiarity is said proverbially to breed contempt, but it may also breed respect. In two ways Jews sought to identify themselves with their neighbours and to resist the legislative efforts to keep them apart. First, they started to take a prominent part in all the revolutionary movements which characterized the eighteenth and nineteenth centuries.

These aimed at destroying the last vestiges of dictatorial and autocratic power and substituting a system of free democratic government. Second, many of them took the easiest way out of their dilemma and became converted to Christianity.

Jew and Christian: the Social Challenge

With regard to the first of these identifications, it is no accident that many who led the new social thinking characteristic of this period were Jews, or at least of Jewish descent. For the whole idea of social reform and the betterment of the human condition emanates from the Hebrew prophets. Indeed, their sublime, passionate appeals such as the one read on the annual Day of Atonement —

> Is not this the fast that I have chosen? to loose the bands of wickedness, to undo the heavy burdens, and to let the oppressed go free, and that ye break every yoke? Is it not to deal thy bread to the hungry, and that thou bring the poor that are cast out to thy house? when thou seest the naked, that thou cover him: and that thou hide not thyself from thine own flesh? —

have penetrated deeply into the Jewish soul and generated a sense of social commitment throughout the ages.

Among the well-known names of those who led this type of political thought in the post-Mendelssohn era are those of Karl Marx and Ferdinand Lassalle. Though the former was baptized at the age of six and, throughout his life, opposed the whole Judaeo-Christian theological outlook, there can be no doubt that his great master-work, *Das Kapital* (sometimes called the Socialist Bible), gave expression in economic terms to the social ethic implicit in both Hebraic prophecy and the teaching of Jesus. Ferdinand Lassalle, on the other hand, did not renounce his Judaism. He devoted his life, cut short through a duel arising from a love affair, to social reform in Germany and became known as one of the founders of the modern Social Democratic movement.

With regard to the second development referred to above, in many cases the forms and beliefs of historic Judaism were shed by these political and cultural leaders, and whole families

(as we have seen in the case of Mendelssohn's descendants)
joined the dominant religion. Sometimes, however, they remained Jews at heart or attempted a kind of synthesis between
Judaism and Christianity. A good instance of this is furnished
by Benjamin Disraeli, the British Prime Minister, who, though
baptized in his infancy, was proud of his descent and deeply
interested in the future of the Jewish people, as we can tell
from his novel *Tancred*. Another was the German poet,
Heinrich Heine, who, graduating in law in 1824 and finding
his religion an insuperable barrier to advancement, submitted
to baptism and became a Protestant. Later he wrote regret-
fully of his conversion:

> I do not make a secret of my Jewish allegiance, to which I
> have not returned, because I have never abjured it. I was
> no apostate from aversion to Judaism. Even symbolically
> I do not consider baptism of any importance, and I shall
> only dedicate myself more entirely to upholding the rights
> of my unhappy brethren. . . I understand very well the
> Psalmist's words: 'Good God, give me my daily bread, that
> I may not blaspheme thy name!'

And in another passage which shows the same sad effort at
self-justification, he states: 'I am proud of the fact that I am
a descendant of those martyrs, who have given a God of morality to the world, and who have fought and suffered on all
the battlefields of thought.' That he should attempt this
identification with those who had stood firm in their faith
despite all pressure indicates both his strange lack of insight
into his personal failure and his confused subconscious
compunction.

Integration

A more dignified type of identification with the general
community became possible when the ghetto disappeared
and all discriminatory laws against the Jewish communities in
the various European states were finally repealed. This consisted in the recognition of Judaism as an official religion.
After the 1848 revolution in France, when the Republic was
restored, Judaism, for the first time in history, was recognized

by the State in the same way as Catholicism and the various Protestant churches. Other countries followed France's example, and from then onwards it became possible for a Jew to be completely integrated into the national and cultural life of his fellow citizens. Gradually, too, he was able to occupy positions of authority and responsibility without having to make any sacrifice of loyalty to his ancestral faith. In Italy, for instance, a Jew was elected Mayor of Rome and another Jew, Luigi Luzzatti, was Prime Minister of Italy between 1910 and 1911. Perhaps the best illustration comes from our own country in the person of Sir Moses Montefiore (1784-1885). As a child he used to play in the garden of his home, East Cliff Lodge, Ramsgate, with the girl who subsequently became Queen Victoria. As he grew older, he became a great philanthropist, helping men and women of all creeds who were in need, and being particularly interested and involved in the welfare of Jews in Palestine. He received many honours, being chosen Sheriff of London and High Sheriff of Kent. He became a Fellow of the Royal Society, and both a Knighthood and a Baronetcy were conferred upon him.

Sir Moses Montefiore's life proved a precedent in Anglo-Jewish circles, and gradually the last official disabilities against Jewish citizens (as well as against Roman Catholics) were removed. In 1858, the last obstruction to full Jewish participation in the country's affairs was abolished with the admission to Parliament of Baron Lionel de Rothschild. Elected Liberal M.P. for the City of London in 1847, he had been barred from taking his seat until the reform of the Oath in 1858. Then at last he was able, with a clear conscience, to swear his allegiance on the Old Testament rather than (as had been demanded of him, and refused, on eleven separate occasions) on the New. A reflection of this was seen in 1871, when Jewish students were finally allowed to receive university degrees without taking an oath which held Christian implications.

14

REFORM IN JUDAISM

Religious Criticism in Germany

We must now take a glance at the effect which emancipation had on the purely religious outlook and practice of those Jews who were now sharing the social, cultural and political life of their fellow citizens in the various countries of Europe. The most marked change came in Germany since it was here that the Haskalah movement started. Adherents of Haskalah (the Hebrew word was coined in 1832 and means 'enlightenment') believed that Jewish emancipation required intellectual and social conformity with non-Jewish communities: they therefore tried to mediate between Orthodoxy and radical assimilation. As a movement it lasted from about 1750 to 1880 and paved the way for Zionism by erecting a stratum of secularized, middle-class Jews soaked in Hebrew culture and abiding by their historic traditions, while at the same time awakened to the political and social ideas of the western world. During this period, it became very clear that the religious practices which had suited the segregated life of the ghetto and absorbed many mystical accretions drawn from Kabbalistic sources and ancient folk-lore no longer catered for a newly emancipated Jewry.

There was, therefore, a need to adapt in two particular ways. First, religion had to satisfy the critical attitude fostered by a new intellectual approach to Judaism. Second, its practice had to be geared to the social habits and cultural life of German society as a whole. Thus the demand arose among the Jewish communities that their religion should be brought up to date in both its theological and ceremonial aspects.

Ceremonial Reform

To understand this we have to get a picture of the kind of social climate which had prevailed during the Middle Ages when the Synagogue had been a central meeting-place for Jewish communal life. It was here that they had felt at home, where they could shake off their minority complex, forget the scorns and insults to which they were subjected in secular life and enjoy social intercourse in a free and friendly atmosphere. These conditions had profoundly affected their attitude to actual worship, which in the period we are considering suffered a temporary deterioration in decorum. Prayers were both lengthy and repetitive. They were entirely in Hebrew, a language increasingly unfamiliar to a growing number of those who had become emancipated (there are similar problems being faced by churches today). Moreover, the atmosphere during the services tended at times to become disorganized and restless — unsuited, it was felt by some, to periods of devotion during the most sacred hours of the individual worshipper's life.

The movement for reform which sprang up as a result of these conditions was influenced to a certain extent by awareness of contemporary Church practices, and this was true not only of Germany but later on of America and this country as well. Jewish reformists demanded shorter forms of service, less repetition, quieter behaviour, and the reading of some prayers as well as the preaching of sermons in the vernacular, whether German or English. Further, there was the introduction of music to beautify the services, and organs came to be built in some synagogues just as in churches, though hitherto it had been forbidden by Jewish law to play any musical instrument on the Sabbath or Festivals. Finally, certain specific prayers dealing with the rebuilding of the Temple, the restoration of the sacrificial system, and the return of Israel to Zion were regarded as obsolete by the reformers and eliminated from the Prayer Book. Zion, they claimed, could be built in any country including, to use the words of one of our poets, in 'England's green and pleasant land'.

Reform Synagogues

The foundation of the first Reform Synagogue came about as the result of a rather special chain of circumstances. A certain Israel Jacobson (1768-1828), President of the Jewish Consistory, which represented Jews in the Napoleonic

kingdom of Westphalia in Germany, was so imbued with the
spirit of social integration characteristic of the times that, in
1801, he founded a boarding-school at Seesen in the Harz
Mountains where Jewish and Christian children were to be
brought up together, as a help towards Jewish-Christian
understanding. Nine years later, Jacobson opened a Reform
Synagogue at Kassel, in association with a similar school which
he founded there. This was modelled on Protestant Church
usage, and, for the first time, hymns were sung to organ
accompaniment, prayers were read in German (as well as in
Hebrew), and girls were confirmed as well as boys in accordance with Church practice. The Jacobson School for Jewish
and Christian pupils existed right up to the Nazi era.

Later, in 1818, a 'Reform Temple' was opened in Hamburg
for adult worshippers, and this became the model for the
many Progressive synagogues built subsequently in Germany
and other countries. In England, the Reform movement
started in 1841. This took the shape of a secession from the
orthodox Sephardi community of Spanish and Portuguese
Jews at the Bevis Marks Synagogue. Following certain internal
reforms, some members of the community petitioned for a
more convenient hour of service, sermons in English, a choir,
and the abolition of a second day of observance following
Holy Days. This was disregarded, and the reformers, not
wishing to secede, asked permission to erect a branch
synagogue where they might institute the desired changes
while the mother synagogue continued along traditional lines.
The request was refused, on grounds of a rule forbidding
such a building within a radius of four miles, and this led
to the formation of an independent congregation in 1840:
the West London Synagogue in Upper Berkeley Street,
London. Since that time, the movement has spread to all
parts of England and the Commonwealth and, today, the
majority of Jewish congregations in the United States have
adopted Reform practice and ritual.

Rejection of the Oral Law
So far the break had been in matters of ritual and observance,
but there followed a more profound cleavage at the theological

level. As has been explained in earlier chapters, traditional
Judaism was based on the Oral Law (Torah) which had been
handed down from generation to generation ever since the
time of the Sinaitic revelation. This was preserved, reinterpreted and sometimes expanded through the great rabbinic
commentaries (e.g. the Talmud) and finally embodied in the
seventeenth-century code, known as the *Shulhan Arukh* (see
p. 50).

The new exponents of Reform now began to question the
validity of the Oral Law and, like the Karaites of old, tended
to look to the Bible itself as their main authority. In Germany,
one of those who advocated basic change was Rabbi Samuel
Holdheim (1806-60), who abolished the observance of the
second day of festivals, and actually persuaded his congregation to transfer the Sabbath to Sunday. He was an opponent
of Talmudic Judaism and his extreme views were disclaimed
even by Reform rabbis, some of whom were of the opinion
that they constituted a negation of Judaism. Rabbi Abraham
Geiger (1810-74), a German theologian and religious reformer,
convened, in 1837, the first conference of Reform rabbis.
Rabbi Isaac Wise (1819-1900), also born in Germany, emigrated to the United States in 1846 and there became 'the
father of Reform Judaism' in America. In 1875, he set up
the Hebrew Union College in Cincinnati which has now
supplied rabbis and ministers for Reform Synagogues throughout the world for almost a century.

This new orientation produced a number of modifications
in traditional Jewish observance which profoundly affected
the whole Jewish way of life in the case of the reformist
sections of the community. Two instances of this far-reaching
change may be given. First the dietary laws which forbade
certain foods such as, for example, pork and bacon, or the
eating of meat and milk at the same meal, were now
considerably modified or even abolished in some Reform
communities. Another instance was the rejection of second-
day observance of each of the festivals. The Jewish calendar
being a lunar one, a two-day observance of festivals had
developed in an age when the exact timing of the New Moon
was not always precisely definable. This ensured that, within

such a span, the festival was correctly dated and timed and
so shared by widely separated communities. This is best
explained by quoting the words of Morris Joseph, an English
Reform minister who published a book early in this century
called *Judaism: Life and Creed*:

> The Second Day Festival owes its origin only to the
> difficulty of ascertaining in pre-scientific times the exact
> dates of the New Moon and the Festivals. But in these
> days, when astronomical events can be calculated before-
> hand with absolute precision, the institution has lost its
> purpose; and even the Synhedrion of old, zealous as it
> was for the maintenance of ancient observances, never
> established the Second Day Festival by formal decree.

This was typical of the arguments used by reformers when
substituting biblical for rabbinic religion. During the nineteenth century the movement spread far and wide, especially
in the United States, and it owed its success partly to the
revolution in thought caused by scientific discovery with all
its implications for ancient theological belief, partly to the
growing desire on the part of Jews to identify themselves
with their contemporary societies and shake off separatist
religious customs. But, not unnaturally, this raised strong
opposition from traditionalists. The whole Reform position
was seriously challenged by the Orthodox, and a great
German philosopher, Samson Raphael Hirsch (1808-88),
used his unrivalled powers of dialectic to show that the old
rabbinic form of Judaism, far from being outworn, had a
profound message and meaning for contemporary life and
contained all that was most valuable in Hebraic tradition.
His strongly expressed view was that the modern generation
should be raised to the Torah and not that the Torah should
be lowered to the generation. Hirsch is regarded as the
progenitor of neo-orthodoxy in western countries, aspiring
to fuse European culture with unqualified loyalty to rigorous-
ly observed traditional Judaism. This conflict in religious
thought has continued right up to the present day.

Judaism as a Missionary Faith

One of the new emphases which came to be made by the reformist school was on the missionary quality of Judaism. The main ground had been prepared for this by the scholar Leopold Zunz, born in Germany in 1794. In the early conflict between Reform and Orthodox communities, Zunz stood midway in his opinions. He inclined towards religious innovation but retained a profound attachment for the historical values of Judaism. He may be regarded as, *par excellence*, the spiritual heir of his compatriot, Moses Mendelssohn. Like his forerunner, he was a man of poor health and limited financial resources, but in the course of a long life (he died in 1886) carried out the roles of journalist, teacher, and preacher. It was he who first realized the significant part which could be played by the study of Judaism in general education, and he strove to get rabbinic literature included in the university curricula of his time.

This led to a consideration of the impact which Judaism might have on the faith and beliefs of the non-Jewish world. In the days of the early Roman empire it had undoubtedly been a missionary faith directed at paganism. This we know from the New Testament (Matt. 23.15): 'you traverse sea and land to make a single proselyte'. There was widespread proselytization, and when even an emperor's wife, Poppaea, had become converted (see p. 36), the Roman senate passed legislation to stop the practice. As a result of this repression and the dangers entailed, together with the rise of Christianity, which by and large took the place of Judaism as a proselytizing faith, the conversionist activities had ceased for some eighteen centuries. The rabbis in the main discouraged proselytes, especially during the period of the mediaeval Church when any attempt at conversion could have led to summary execution. They gradually evolved the theory that while the Moral Law as summarized in the so-called Noachic principles (see p. 18) was for all mankind, the Ceremonial Law, that is the practice and discipline of institutional Judaism, was for the Jewish people alone.

With the emancipation, however, there was a fresh orientation of Jewish universalism and commitment. Reform Jews,

and especially the later Liberals, began to hark back to those
deeply moving passages in the second Isaiah which described
Israel's future role as that of a 'suffering servant', chastized
for the sins of the whole human race, and to interpret the
destiny of the Jewish people in redemptive terms.

C. G. Montefiore

The pioneer in this secondary stage of reform was an English
Liberal Jew named Claude Montefiore. In his youth he had
studied under the great Jowett, Master of Balliol College,
Oxford, and, following the Balliol tradition, he became a
philosopher as well as a theologian, and this shaped his whole
approach to Judaism. In fact it may be said that he gave a
kind of direction to the reformist movement in this country
similar to that which Moses Mendelssohn had given in
Germany.

To him the Jewish faith was a universal one, transcending
national barriers, and he felt himself to be fully an Englishman
as well as a Jew. He went even further than the early
reformers in emphasizing the missionary role of Israel and
thought that not only the teachings of Judaism, but also the
ceremonial, must be adapted in some way to make it
acceptable to all. Here are his actual words:

> Religion, both in doctrine and ceremonial, should be
> something super-national. It should bind races and nations
> together, and it should not keep them sundered and apart.
> It is not sufficient to offer to outsiders excellent doctrines
> without also offering to them forms and ceremonial.
> Religion is a whole, and the doctrines need a form. Men
> cannot do with doctrines (however excellent) alone. They
> require an historic ceremonial as well. Judaism must offer
> them both. (C.G. Montefiore, *Outlines of Liberal Judaism*,
> ch. 12, p. 168)

Liberal Judaism and Progressive Revelation

It has been shown earlier in this chapter that there was some
resemblance between the line taken by the earliest reformers
and that of the Karaites. In rejecting the Oral Law the latter

had gone back to the Written Law, to the Bible itself, and regarded this (in what today would be called fundamentalist terms) as being in its totality the 'word of God' and so the divinely inspired authority for Judaism. The events describing the giving of the Law on Mount Sinai were accepted as historical fact, as representing a final and complete revelation of God to his people Israel. Even the mediaeval philosopher Maimonides, in drawing up the Thirteen Principles of the Jewish faith, stated his ninth principle as follows: 'I believe with perfect faith that this Law will not be changed, and that there will never be any other law from the Creator, blessed be His name.'

But in the nineteenth century there were two developments which brought about far-reaching changes in religious thought. The first was the new scientific theory of evolution, first propounded by Darwin, which appeared completely to falsify the fundamental concept of creation as described in the opening chapters of Genesis. The second was the application of what is called 'higher criticism' to the text of the Bible. This, in essence, meant that the biblical books were subjected to the same critical process as any other literature, and problems of authorship, veracity and so on were discussed in the light of literary and historical research. This led to the rejection of many hitherto accepted views about the text of the Bible such as the Mosaic authorship of the whole Pentateuch or that a single prophet composed the whole book of Isaiah.

The later reformers adopted both these critical attitudes and no longer regarded the whole Bible or even the whole Torah as divinely inspired. Nor did they think that divine revelation was limited to the Bible or the biblical age. This was put with great clarity and succinctness by Morris Joseph in his book, *Judaism as Creed and Life:*

Revelation is the communication of God's will to man. And such a communication is made to every human being. It is implied in the very possession of a moral sense, in our conception of ourselves as moral beings . . . For us Jews the Bible contains the most sacred communication of the

Divine commands. But it is not the only revelation of God that man possesses. There are millions of human beings who have never seen the Bible, never even heard of it. Shall we say that God left them without the means of learning His will? Surely not. Some of those huge multitudes have Scriptures of their own, which, though they contain much that we cannot accept, still are like our Bible inasmuch as they teach the duty of goodness, and teach it in God's name. They are, therefore, a revelation of the Supreme, a means divinely ordained for the moral education of the human race.

This train of thought was further developed by some modern Jewish theologians (particularly of the Liberal outlook) and embodied in the doctrine of what is called Progressive Revelation, a doctrine which goes to the root of the nature of ultimate truth and comes to terms with the theory of evolution referred to above. According to its viewpoint, man progresses as God reveals his nature and purpose to him throughout the time process. This does not deny that some final and unalterable things have been said through the Bible and other works at specific periods in the past: 'He has showed you, O man, what is good' (Mic. 6.8). But it does mean that no man or generation has yet unravelled the total mystery of life and creation or penetrated into the profundity of God's nature. This remains to be disclosed in the fullness of time.

The Liberal Jewish Community

Just as Reform Judaism in this country began as a secession from Orthodox, so Liberal Judaism started as a breakaway from Reform. The origins go back to 1902, when a distinguished woman scholar and social worker, the Hon. Lily A. Montagu, founded a body called the Jewish Religious Union, together with C. G. Montefiore and Israel Abrahams (see below). At first this new group was at least recognized by both Orthodox and Reform Jewish leaders, but eventually the Liberals formed their own separate community: they acquired a building in 1910 and in 1912 brought over Rabbi

Dr Israel Mattuck from New York to lead them; in 1925, they moved to St John's Wood, which is still the headquarters of Liberal Judaism.

The Liberal belief, as we have seen, is in the progressive revelation of God's will in each generation. Thus, the complete authority of the Written and the Oral Laws is not followed, but the ancient teaching is linked with a modern approach which encourages individuals to make personal decisions.

Liberal services, as do Reform, differ in a marked degree from those of the Orthodox community. In the Synagogue, men and women sit together, head-covering being optional. Services are short, being partly in Hebrew, partly in English, and many modern prayers replace those of the traditional Prayer Book. As with Reform, travelling on the Sabbath is permitted. The Dietary Laws may be observed or not, as the individual wishes (the Reform community is here more meticulous though some congregations are left to their own conscience). Ritual and ceremonial are thought of not as God-given but more as a 'visual aid', strongly to be recommended. Second-day observance has been abolished. In all these matters of practice, the Reform community stands slightly nearer the Orthodox than does the Liberal.

New Attitudes towards Christianity

One of the great services rendered to Jewry by C. G. Montefiore and other Jewish scholars of his time was to create a better understanding of Christianity. In mediaeval times, as we have seen, there had been some attempts at 'dialogue' between exponents of the two faiths, and Maimonides had actually written that 'Christianity has done more to spread the Bible than Judaism itself'. But the partners in these dialogues were never on an equal footing, and the truth of Christianity with its corollary, the falsity of Judaism, was assumed by the judges before the confrontation started. Further, memories of the Crusades, the Inquisition, and ghetto life had so hardened the Jewish mind against Christianity that to most Jews the New Testament was a closed book.

What Montefiore and his followers did was to open this

book for Jewish readers and show them how closely related
the two religions were. Another book, written in conjunction
with a Cambridge scholar, Israel Abrahams (also a Liberal
Jew), was a commentary on the Synoptic Gospels, and this
showed both Jews and Christians how much the New
Testament owed to the Hebrew Bible and rabbinic teaching.

A parallel service was rendered by a number of Christian
writers, such as George Foot Moore and Travers Herford, who
tried to rid the Christian mind of its illusion that the new
dispensation as conveyed through the New Testament had
rendered the old one obsolete and irrelevant. Herford even
went so far as to defend the Pharisees and clear their reputation from some of the imputations made against them. Quite
recently, a distinguished Anglican minister and scholar, the
Revd Dr James Parkes, has propounded the view that the
two faiths are not mutually exclusive but rather com-
plementary.

This new understanding has been further developed in our
own day by Jewish writers, both Orthodox and Liberal,
especially in the United States. It finds its fullest expression
in a book by a Jewish scholar named Martin Buber called *Two
Types of Faith*. In it, he propounds the original theory that
while Christianity rests on the principle of belief, acceptance
of something new — he uses the Greek word *Pistis* — Judaism
is a religion of trust (*Emunah*) based on historical experience.
It is in the person of Jesus that he finds a kind of convergence
between the two views:

> From my youth onwards I have found in Jesus my great
> brother. That Christianity has regarded and does regard
> him as God and Saviour has always appeared to me a fact
> of the highest importance which, for his sake and my own,
> I must endeavour to understand. . . I am more than ever
> certain that a great place belongs to him in Israel's history
> of faith. . .

Those Christians who have thus far followed the development of 'breakaway' communities — Reform and Liberal —
will immediately recognize the similarity of pattern within
the Jewish faith to the rise of Free Church communities

within the Christian faith. What needs to be borne in mind is that the bitterness (even enmity and persecution) directed towards some of the Free Churches took place mainly in the seventeenth, eighteenth and early nineteenth centuries (though some denominations go back into the sixteenth). Nowadays, on the principle of time being a great healer, we find that those old animosities have died away. Indeed, a quite new climate of thinking has developed, in which the great bodies within the Christian faith are drawing steadily closer and — so far as is possible without compromising their special beliefs — acting together in concord upon major issues which confront the world today. This can be seen in the work of such organizations as the World Council of Churches.

Perhaps this may be a pattern which will emerge within the Jewish faith, too. But here we have to understand that, for Jews, it is today rather as it was with Christians in earlier centuries. Most Jewish communities, whatever their outlook, are still too close to divisive internal events to be able to view close 'fraternizing' with equanimity — without a wary anxiety or even open rejection. This is natural and understandable. We may, however, hope that the more rapid and accelerating pace of toleration, so notable in religious affairs throughout the world today, will have its eventual effect also on the various shades of opinion within the Jewish community.

15

THE ZIONIST MOVEMENT

In History

All through Jewish history there has been a longing among a
large section of the people for a return to the Holy Land and
the city of Jerusalem — particularly to Mount Zion, which
furnished this heartfelt aspiration with 'a local habitation
and a name'. This longing had its roots in ancient Hebrew
prophecy, particularly those passages with a Messianic implication such as the following:

> It shall come to pass in the latter days that the mountain
> of the house of the Lord shall be established as the highest
> of the mountains, and shall be raised above the hills; and
> all the nations shall flow to it, and many peoples shall
> come, and say: 'Come, let us go up to the mountain of the
> Lord, to the house of the God of Jacob; that he may teach
> us his ways and that we may walk in his paths.' For out of
> Zion shall go forth the law, and the word of the Lord
> from Jerusalem. (Isa. 2.2-3)

There are even more specific prophecies of a return of the
Jewish people from the countries of the Diaspora, and these
had a profound influence on the later Zionist movements:

> Fear not, for I am with you; I will bring your offspring
> from the east, and from the west I will gather you; I will
> say to the north, Give up, and to the south, Do not
> withhold; bring my sons from afar and my daughters from
> the end of the earth. . . (Isa. 43.5-6)

Similar hopes are expressed in many of the Psalms and are
still in current use in the Jewish Prayer Book. Here, for
instance, is the 126th Psalm, sung after meals on the Sabbath
and Jewish Festivals:

> When the Lord turned again the captivity of Zion,
> we were unto them that dream.

Then was our mouth filled with laughter,
and our tongue with singing;
then said they among the nations,
'The Lord hath done great things for them.'
The Lord hath done great things for us;
whereof we are glad.
Turn again our captivity, O Lord,
As the streams in the South.
They that sow in tears shall reap in joy!
Though he goeth on his way weeping, bearing forth the seed
He shall come again with joy, bringing his sheaves with him.

And there is the forlorn passage from Psalm 137 expressing the feeling of an outcast:

How shall we sing the Lord's song,
In a strange land?
If I forget thee, O Jerusalem,
Let my right hand forget her cunning.
Let my tongue cleave to the roof of my mouth,
If I remember thee not;
If I prefer not Jerusalem
Above my chief joy!   (Ps. 137.4-6)

Among prayer-book passages which sound the same note and are still recited daily in Orthodox homes and synagogues, the following may be quoted: 'O bring us in peace from the four corners of the earth, and make us go upright to our land; for thou art a God who worketh salvation. . .' and 'Sound the great horn for our freedom; lift up the ensign to gather our exiles, and gather us from the four corners of the earth. Blessed art thou, O Lord, who gatherest the banished ones of thy people Israel.' Finally, as we have seen, the longing for a return to Zion was reflected in the work of mediaeval Jewish writers such as Judah Ha-Levi (see p.64) who wrote:

In the East, in the East is my heart, and I dwelt at the end of the West,
How shall I join your feasting, how shall I share in your jest?

In spite of this, the Reform section of world Jewry — and this applies to some of the Orthodox as well — tended to reject these particularist or nationalistic aspirations in Judaism and regarded the dispersion (Diaspora) of the Jewish people as an essential factor in the carrying out of their divine mission — their Messianic role among all the nations of the earth. They went even so far as to delete all references to a return of the exiles to Mount Zion from their prayer book. This attitude was expressed with great conviction and clarity in Morris Joseph's book *Judaism as Creed and Life*: (p.170):

> They [the non-Zionists] cannot believe in the Restoration of the Jewish State for they hold that such an event would impede rather than promote the fulfilment of the great purpose for which Israel exists. The moral and religious education of the world, they maintain, can best be promoted by close contact between Jew and Gentile. Isolation, they argue, even though it be isolation in Palestine and accompanied by national independence, would mean failure for Israel's mission. Those who hold this opinion point in justification to the memorable saying of the Rabbis . . . that the dispersion of the Jew over the earth was providentially designed as a means of winning the world for religious truth.

Messianic and Political Zionism

This whole concept, however, which was based on the theory of political assimilation — Judaism being regarded as a religion without nationalist ties or implications — was seriously shaken by a number of developments which took place in Europe at the end of the nineteenth and the beginning of the twentieth centuries. Today, we tend more and more to accept the principle of cultural and racial diversity as essential to the well-being and harmony of any civilized society, though there are still those who resist 'the wind of change', to use Mr Macmillan's phrase when he drew attention to the position accorded to coloured people in South Africa.

In the period we are considering, it looked as though the policy of emancipation adopted by so many European states would solve the problems of minority groups such as the

Jews. In 1855, for instance, the most tolerant of Russian monarchs, Alexander II, ascended the throne and attempted to bring about the integration of Jewish citizens by education and the gradual relaxation of restrictions. In Poland, a revolutionary uprising of 1863 proclaimed equal rights for Jews and, although the uprising was suppressed in the following year, there was left in its wake a certain tendency towards assimilation; Jews now held key positions in foreign trade, industry, finance, and the free professions. Rumania, itself granted complete independence under the Treaty of Berlin (1878), agreed (under pressure from western European Jewry) to a clause within the Treaty which gave political rights and equality to Rumanian Jews.

But, as so often happened in history, a violent reaction set in against these humanitarian policies, and a calculated wave of antisemitism, reminiscent of the Middle Ages, swept through a number of countries. In Russia, after the assassination of Alexander II, Jews suffered some of the worst cruelties to which they had ever been subjected. The appalling pogroms of the 1880s led to the official view that Jews were a foreign element, to be kept apart from the rural population. Protests from western Europe were in vain, and a vast exodus to England and America began at the turn of the century. Russian Jewry showed, in that period, some of the most vital qualities of the Jewish people. It offered, together with Poland, the world's greatest centres of Talmudic study; it was a focus of Hebrew literary revival, and it produced many of the remarkable historic figures of Zionism. But the steady deterioration of conditions under which Jews could live in Russia made the enormous waves of emigration inevitable. The notorious 'May Laws' of 1882, forbidding Jews to settle or acquire property outside the towns, or to move from place to place, also gave — quite apart from disabilities — a tremendous impetus to Hebrew nationalism.

In Poland, conditions rapidly became similar. Church, press, and the majority of political groups supported a campaign against Jewish citizens which led to a pogrom in Warsaw in 1881. Rumania, after reluctant acceptance of political rights and equality for Rumanian Jews, ruthlessly ignored the clause to which she had agreed in the Treaty of Berlin, reverting to an active antisemitic policy which was termed by the United States representative in Paris 'a disgrace to Christian civilization'.

Because of this denial of citizenship in so many European countries, the age-long demand on the part of a section of the Jewish people that they should have a home and a national life of their own received a fresh and dramatic impetus. The old Messianic dream of a return to Mount Zion, the rebuilding of the Temple and the ushering in of an age which would bring salvation to all mankind became crystallized in the form of an urgent political movement. In the case of some thinkers the two ideas were blended: as with Asher Ginsberg (1856-1927), best known under his pen-name of Ahad Ha-am ('one of the people'). Ginsberg was born in the Ukraine of a Hasidic family. In 1886 he settled in Odessa, where he occupied a leading position in the Palestine movement and in Hebrew publishing. In 1908, he moved to London, and in 1922 to Tel Aviv, where he died a few years later. In his writings, Ginsberg sought to give an ethico-sociological foundation to the Jewish national idea. The revival of the Jewish nation must involve the revival of Judaism; it had to be a morally based 'spiritual Zionism':

Now the material settlement admittedly has a bearing on our spiritual problem, and is indeed necessary to its full solution. I would go further, and say that in my opinion the whole point of the material settlement — whether its architects realize it or not — is to provide the foundation for that spiritual centre of our nation which is destined to arise in Palestine in response to the insistent urge of the national instinct. . . We Jews are not a new-born nation, just beginning to climb the ladder of progress rung by rung. We climbed the lower rungs of the ladder thousands of years ago, and had reached a high level of culture when our natural progress was forcibly arrested. The ground was cut away from under our feet, and we were left hanging in mid-air, carrying a valuable load of accumulated culture, but without any sort of basis for healthy life or free development. So things went on for centuries. The Jewish people remained miserably poised between heaven and earth, struggling with all its might to preserve its cultural inheritance and not to fall below the level it had reached in the more prosperous days. And now, when we have some hope of coming down to earth again and building our life on solid natural foundations, are we to be told that we ought to jettison our burden of culture so as to be better able to concentrate on the material tasks which normally take precedence, and afterwards start again, in the customary fashion, at the bottom of the ladder?

(*Essays, Translated by Leon Simon*)

Revival of Antisemitism

The change of outlook in Europe following the Emancipation movement led to the backlash of antisemitism described above, but on the whole this assumed new forms which were not at first characterized by violence and persecution as in the old unhappy days of the mediaeval Church. In some ways, however, it was a more insidious form of antisemitism, at least in Germany and Austria where it originated. Here, though theoretically all restrictions against Jews had been abolished, there was a deliberate campaign, particularly after the Franco-Prussian war in 1870, to keep Jews out of public life and the higher grades of education. This resulted from a spirit of chauvinism with its emphasis on a jingoistic form of nationalism and the almost mythical concept of racial purity.

Characteristically, it led to the formation of antisemitic parties who used all the resources of a most bitter and virulent propaganda to denigrate Jews as a degenerate and subversive race. Old calumnies were revived such as the Blood Libel, which accused Jews of killing Christian children for purposes of sacrifice at the Passover festival. There appeared at the same time a new antisemitic document, now proved to be a forgery, which has been widely circulated right up to the present day. This was the *Protocols of the Elders of Zion*, which purported to show that Jews were plotting to overthrow the government of every country and to establish a world supremacy for themselves.

Propaganda of this kind, especially when it endorses popular prejudice, is apt to have far-reaching and disastrous consequences. In the case of the Jewish people it led to two important developments which profoundly influenced their future history. One was what has come to be known as the 'Dreyfus Affair'. This took place in France in 1894, when a Jewish captain in the French army, Alfred Dreyfus, was accused of selling military secrets to the Germans. Though completely innocent (the false accusation was based on the forgery of a French officer, Major Esterhazy, serving in the German secret service), Dreyfus was publicly degraded and sent off to Devil's Island to serve a sentence of life imprisonment. The French people were divided into Dreyfusards and anti-Dreyfusards, and it was owing to the protests of the latter and especially Zola's famous declaration *J'accuse* that, after four years, Dreyfus was recalled to Paris and subsequently set free through the intervention of the French President. He was entirely rehabilitated, resumed his career in the army, and eventually retired with the rank of Lieutenant-Colonel. The 'Dreyfus Affair' not only stirred and divided France: the clergy, the military and the right-wing politicians refused to recognize a miscarriage of justice, which would have lowered the prestige of the army, and supported their position by exploiting latent antisemitism. Their refusal had its repercussions later in the separation of Church and State in France (1905), in the rise of the Socialist Party, and in the growth of the Zionist movement throughout Jewry.

A second development at this time which contributed so greatly to the future history of the Jewish people was the upsurge of antisemitism in Russia following the assassination of Alexander II. As we have seen, the disabilities imposed on Jewish citizens made life insupportable and led to wave upon wave of emigration. Not only did Jews in Russia suffer from severe restrictions, but the Cossacks were deliberately inflamed against them and, time and again, charged into the Jewish quarters of towns and villages to inflict wholesale massacre on the inhabitants. The worst atrocities occurred in Kiev and Odessa in 1881 and, as a result of these pogroms, tens of thousands were rendered homeless and destitute and forced to leave their native land. Large numbers of them, both at this time and in the early years of the twentieth century, sought refuge in Great Britain and America, and their descendants still form a considerable proportion of the western Jewish communities.

As a result of this early emigration, we find that the United States today (1970 figures) has the largest Jewish community in the world, totalling well over five million. That in the Soviet Union, though drastically depleted, takes second place today, with about 2,600,000. Significantly, third place is held by Israel, totalling over 2,500,000. It is clear that the drastic changes of Jewish population in Russia at the turn of the century have had immense consequences for world Jewry through the development and concentration of large free communities in both Israel and, predominantly, the United States.

Theodor Herzl

It was the Dreyfus case that caused a deeply emotional reaction in the heart of a young Jewish Austrian journalist, Theodor Herzl, who had hitherto felt himself completely assimilated into his national culture and on whom Judaism, as a faith, had ceased to have serious impact. After leaving the court where Dreyfus was tried, and hearing the anti-Jewish cries of the French crowd outside, he had come to the conclusion that the only way in which the Jewish problem could be solved was by a revival of nationalism and the establishment of a new Jewish state in Palestine, the land of their ancestors.

In this he had the support of large numbers of eastern Jewry and particularly of an earlier movement among Russian Jews called *Hovevei Zion* ('Lovers of Zion') who had witnessed the complete failure of Haskalah or cultural integration in their country. But where Jewish communities were more happily entrenched in the total society, as in Great Britain, he encountered strong opposition. This came not only from Reform Jews but from many of the Orthodox as well, who conceived the 'Return to Zion' not in political terms, but as a far-off, divine, Messianic event.

Further, a parallel solution to the Jewish problem was put forward by a section of Jews in this country which sought to find a Jewish homeland in some other part of the world in view of the difficulties involved in turning Palestine, largely an Arab country at this time ruled by the Turks, into a Jewish state. Israel Zangwill (1864-1926), an English novelist and man of letters, born in London of Russian parents, took up this aspect of the cause of Zionism with enthusiasm. It was Zangwill's success in a new field of 'local colour' writing with his first Jewish book, *Children of the Ghetto*, which caused him to devote himself more and more to Jewish affairs. At one period he advocated the settlement of Jews in Uganda, but this scheme came to nothing — mainly, of course, because for Jews the 'promised land' had always been Palestine. A second factor in Zangwill's efforts on behalf of persecuted Jewry was his association with Herzl and the influence which Herzl exerted over his thinking.

Herzl (1860-1904) was the true founder of political Zionism. In contrast to Aḥad Ha-am, and against the view prevailing among western Jews that Jews were solely a religious community, he declared: 'We are a nation, a nation.' And he demanded for this nation a territory for the building up of a Jewish state. Through his involvement in the Jewish students' union in Vienna, Herzl became the leader of the Zionist movement; he founded the Zionist newspaper, *Die Welt* (though his own newspaper, *Die Neue Freie Presse*, kept silent over his Zionist activities, of which its Jewish owners disapproved); he convened the First Zionist Congress in Basle in August 1897. Here he managed to gain general support for the foundation of a legally secured national home for the Jewish people in Palestine. And it was here in Basle that the World Zionist Organization was initiated, of which Herzl, presiding over six subsequent Zionist Congresses, remained President until his death. The sixth of these Congresses was notable for the storm of protest at the news that Britain had approved of Jewish settlement in Uganda, and evoked Herzl's declaration that Palestine remained the ultimate aim. It was this storm, coming after his unremitting efforts for Zionism, and his ceaseless travels to enlist sympathetic support from heads of states, which affected his already weakened heart, so that he died in 1904 at Edlach in Austria. In 1949, his remains were reinterred on Mt Herzl, to the west of Jerusalem.

Actually, in spite of a good deal of obstruction that it encountered from the more assimilated Jew, Theodor Herzl's
campaign on behalf of the political Zionist movement achieved
amazing success. He himself was an attractive and persuasive
speaker with a dynamic personality. He was young when he
died — only forty-four — but the fruits of his labour can be
seen in the creation and present existence of the State of
Israel.

The Balfour Declaration

But what of the country of Palestine itself and the nature of
its inhabitants at this time? Had the Jewish people any legal
or moral justification for claiming it as their own?

The latter question, a searching one, especially today, does
not admit of any simple or generally accepted answers. As we
have seen, since 1513 Palestine had been part of the Turkish
empire. It was, therefore, a Moslem country largely inhabited
by Arabs, but the Jewish claim rested on a unique and un-
broken historical relationship. Jews had always lived there
and, as described in a previous chapter, many western Jews
such as Judah Ha-Levi and Nahmanides regarded it as their
spiritual home and even ended their days there. Thus, as James
Parkes has stressed in a booklet published after the 1967 Arab-
Israeli war (*Arabs and Jews in the Middle East: a Tragedy of
Errors*), there was never any period from the time of Joshua
onwards when this particular land was entirely without Jewish inhabitants.

This fact must be taken into account when we come to
consider the kind of recognition which has been accorded in
recent years to intensive Jewish claims with regard to the land
of Palestine and all the events, happy and otherwise, to which
such recognition gave rise. The first concrete step in the reassertion of this relationship was taken by Great Britain at
the end of the First World War. During this war thousands of
Jews had fought and died side by side with their non-Jewish
fellow citizens for the allied cause, and the loyalty of English
Jews to this country was dramatically expressed by an Anglo-
Jewish poetess, Alice Lucas:

For the Jew has heart and hand, our Mother England,
And they both are thine today —
Thine for life and thine for death — yea, thine forever!
Wilt thou take them as we give them freely, gladly?
England, say!

Great service, too, was rendered to the allied cause by an
Anglo-Jewish scientist, Dr Chaim Weizmann, a lecturer at
Manchester University, whose discoveries in the field of
explosives were of very great assistance to the allied powers,
while his researches into organic chemistry earned him an
international reputation. After Herzl's death, Weizmann, who
opposed the Uganda scheme of settlement, supported a kind
of 'synthetic' Zionism which tried to unite the practical work
of colonization in Palestine with political and diplomatic
activity. He became the Chairman of the London committee
within the Zionist movement, and then in 1920 President of
the Zionist Organization, an office he held until 1931 and
again from 1935.

It was Weizmann's influence, during the First World War,
and the impact of his personality on leading British statesmen,
which succeeded in securing recognition of Palestine as 'the
national home of the Jewish people'. Thus it was in a spirit of
reciprocity that Britain was, to some extent, won over
to Zionism — a development which was given practical expression in what is known as 'The Balfour Declaration'.
When General Allenby liberated Jerusalem from the Turk on
10 December 1917, Lord Balfour, the Foreign Secretary,
issued the following declaration, finally approved by the
British Cabinet, and sent to Lord (Walter) Rothschild who
was asked to convey it to the Zionist Federation:

Foreign Office
November 2nd, 1917

Dear Lord Rothschild,
    I have much pleasure in conveying to you, on behalf
of His Majesty's Government, the following declaration of
sympathy with Jewish Zionist aspirations, which has been
submitted to, and approved by, the Cabinet.

'His Majesty's Government view with favour the establishment in Palestine of a national home for the Jewish people, and will use their best endeavours to facilitate the achievement of this object, it being clearly understood that nothing shall be done which may prejudice the civil and religious rights of existing non-Jewish communities in Palestine, or the rights and political status enjoyed by Jews in any other country.'

I should be pleased if you would bring this declaration to the knowledge of the Zionist Federation.

Yours sincerely,

ARTHUR JAMES BALFOUR

This declaration was endorsed by both France and America, and as a result, when a peace treaty came to be drawn up at the end of hostilities and Palestine became a mandatory country under the new League of Nations, the mandate was handed over to Great Britain. Lord (formerly Sir Herbert) Samuel, who had been Postmaster-General in the Liberal Government under Asquith, was appointed High Commissioner of the country, and a Jewish Agency representing the Zionist movement became the recognized authority for re-establishing Jewish life in the ancestral home. It was during this period that Chaim Weizmann, as Chairman of the Zionist Commission which went to Palestine in 1918, did so much to prepare the way for initiating the Jewish National Home. In 1918 he laid the cornerstone of the Hebrew University; in 1919, represented the Zionist movement at the peace conference; in 1920, convened the London Zionist Conference to mobilize support for work in Palestine.

There followed an almost miraculous transformation of a country which for so many centuries had lain dormant and under-developed. The number of Jewish inhabitants rose from 55,000 in 1918 to 450,000 in 1939. A new industrial city was built, Tel Aviv, and gradually the barren soil became fertilized through the labour of a number of agricultural settlers and pioneers (Halutzim). Later, this work was helped forward through the establishment of communal settlements, known as Kibbutzim (*Kibbutz* = 'gathering-in'), some religious in character, some purely secular. These owed their origin to the communist settlements in Eastern Europe and further back, perhaps, to the ideas contained in Plato's *Republic*. The family system was in many cases discarded in favour of a collectivized society in which children were brought up in common, and all members shared the domestic, administrative and agricultural tasks. In the case of the Kibbutzim founded on Israel's borders there was also military training, and they rendered great service to the country, protecting it from the raids of Arab neighbours.

It must be borne in mind, however, that in spite of this astonishing rebirth of Jewish life on Palestinian soil, the foundation of a 'national home for the Jewish people' and subsequently of a Jewish state has not proved to be an unmixed blessing. The fact is that the Balfour Declaration promised two incompatible things, and the whole Zionist policy in Palestine was violently opposed by its Arab inhabitants who were still, at that time, in the vast majority. They always maintained that they were far from being anti-Jewish but that the establishment of a national home for Jews was an infringement of their rights as guaranteed in the Declaration itself. This has been the main cause of the unhappy situation which still exists today in the Middle East.

Nazi Persecution and Growth of Jewish Nationalism
History is always unpredictable, and it was just at this turning-point in the history of the Jewish people that they were subjected to the worst form of persecution that they had ever endured. This came about as the result of the rise of Hitler in 1933, a subject which cannot be given adequate treatment from either the psychological or political angle in a single section of a short history textbook, but which requires to be studied from the vast literature available as a subject in its own right. What should be noted here is that the German dictator, during the period of the Third Reich, became obsessed with the false racial concepts of a French sociologist called Gobineau, who taught that human races were basically unequal, the white race — especially the Nordic — being essentially superior. Hitler was able to indoctrinate his party,

the Nazis, who subsequently held total power in Germany, with the theory that the Jews were the cause of Germany's defeat in the First World War and that, if they were to 'preserve Germany for pure Germans', they must first wipe out the Jewish people which, he asserted, infected the body politic of their Nordic nation.

Actually, as we have seen, the Jewish community was more deeply integrated in the national life in Germany than in any other country: Jews had, in fact, settled in the Rhineland before Germans came to what is now known as Germany. Yet Hitler succeeded in winning over the majority of his fellow countrymen to this pernicious doctrine. Some courageous individuals protested, but on the whole even those who were anti-Nazi followed the line of least resistance, silence giving consent. In 1935 the Nuremberg laws were passed, which removed all civil rights from Jewish citizens, and later, through a policy of extermination, efficiently organized and ruthlessly prosecuted, their homes and property were attacked, their synagogues and cemeteries desecrated, and they themselves sent in train-loads to the concentration camps and gas chambers. When the Second World War started in 1939 and Germany spread her conquests over Europe, persecution of the Jewish communities was actively fostered in other countries (for instance, Poland and Hungary), and a reign of terror was instituted during which almost the whole of European Jewry was destroyed. Nearly six million Jews died — about one-third of the total number in the world.

As may be imagined, these terrible events led to a marked change in the Jewish attitude all over the world towards the Zionist or nationalist concept. It was felt, firstly, that refugees from persecution must be given a new, secure national life and, secondly, that in a hostile world Jews would never be safe unless they became a nation like other nations in a land of their own. Thus the opposition to the Zionist solution, though still maintained by some on religious or Messianic grounds, tended to disappear in the face of a physical threat to their whole existence.

State of Israel

There followed a period of conflict and turbulence in the
Middle East which has lasted right up to the present day. It
started with the problem raised by countless Jewish refugees
fleeing from the holocaust in Nazi Germany. Though sections
of these were given asylum in many western countries, notably
England and America, they tragically failed — owing to Arab
opposition — to gain admission into the 'Jewish national
home'. Great Britain, the mandatory power, was faced with a
complex situation, and successive British governments vacil-
lated in their Palestinian policy. In 1937 and again in 1947
proposals to partition Palestine were rejected as unworkable.
In 1939 a conference in London considered the creation of an
independent Palestine free of the British mandate, but this
was refused by Dr Weizmann since it envisaged a permanent
Arab majority. After the war, restriction on Jewish immigra-
tion led to violent anti-British attacks by Jewish terrorist gangs,
and finally, in May 1948, Britain relinquished the mandate.
This led to the proclamation by the Palestinian Jews of the
State of Israel, and though it was immediately attacked by all
the surrounding Arab peoples, it gained an astonishing victory
and succeeded in establishing itself, finally gaining membership of the United Nations.

During the subsequent years, the Jewish population in-
creased to 2,500,000. They succeeded in building up a
remarkable national life, assimilated large numbers of refugees
from many different countries and ethnic groups, reclaimed
vast tracts of barren soil, fostered industry and commerce,
established friendly relations with the majority of foreign
nations and created cultural institutions in the arts, sciences,
technology and general education. The Hebrew University at
Jerusalem gained universal recognition in academic circles,
and the technological training received by students, especially
at the Haifa Technion, enabled them to bring technical aid to
a number of under-developed countries, particularly in the
African continent.

The state of war between Israel and the bordering Arab
states has, however, gone on right up to the present day. This
situation was exacerbated by the flight of thousands of Arab

refugees from their Palestinian homes, and these, particularly in the Gaza strip, have constituted a permanent problem, exploited in many cases by the various Arab governments who refused to receive them in their own states. The borders of the new State of Israel varied considerably from those originally envisaged and, though a United Nations force was posted on them, this failed to stop innumerable border raids from the Arab countries with subsequent Israeli reprisals conducted with considerable bitterness on a large scale. Finally, the city of Jerusalem, which was to have been international according to the edict of the United Nations, remained divided between Israel and Jordan until 1967 with all the restrictions associated with an iron curtain — in this case, the Mandelbaum Gate between the two parts of the city.

Suez and the Six Day War

This was the situation that prevailed until actual warfare broke out between Israel and her Arab neighbours on three occasions during the present period. The first clash consisted of a preventive war started by the Israelis in 1956 in order to forestall aggressive action planned by the Egyptians and the United Arab Republic under the leadership of President Nasser, evidence of which had been furnished through the concentration of arms and forces in the Sinai peninsula. When Nasser nationalized the Suez Canal in 1954, eliminating Britain and France from its management, he precipitated an international crisis. Israel saw in this an opportunity to settle her score with Egypt and to halt border attacks — even to achieve some sort of eventual peace. The fierce debate within the Israeli government came down finally in favour of hard-line action against the Egyptians, and this was supported by Britain and France. It was largely through the successful British air attacks on the Egyptian airfields that Israel was able to advance across the Sinai peninsula and destroy the Egyptian military concentrations. As the result, however, of United Nations intervention, there was a complete withdrawal of the invading forces and the former boundaries were re-established.

The second clash is known as the 'Six Day War' which took place in June 1967. This time Nasser started warlike action, first by occupying the Gulf of Akaba and refusing to let Israeli ships pass to the port of Elath, second by insisting that the United Nations force be removed from the border. He was supported by both Jordan and Syria who, together with Egypt, saw a golden opportunity for the total liquidation of the Israeli state. It should, as a matter of historical fact, be noted that it was the Arab forces which took the initial step of unleashing the Six Day War, and not, as is often inaccurately believed, the State of Israel. A letter from Mr Aharon Remez, at that time the Israeli Ambassador in Great Britain, appeared in the *Guardian* on 6 June 1967 and dealt with the technically important question of 'who fired the first shot' — important in relation to the obligations of the United Nations Charter. It is clear from this letter that Israel was invaded in the early hours of the 5th, and immediately put into operation her plan of defence. In the *Daily Telegraph* of 15 June, a report from Egyptian officers captured during the war said that their 'operation in the Gaza Strip which began the war was only a probe of Israeli defences, and was not intended to penetrate more than ten miles'. The report, however, added revealingly: 'It would have been followed later by a drive which should have reached Tel Aviv in twenty-four hours.' This 'probing' operation brought from the Israelis a well-planned retaliatory action, so that they very soon occupied not only the Sinai desert, but also the West Bank of the Jordan, the Arab quarter of Jerusalem, and the heights on the Syrian side of the border which so crucially overlook their country.

Since 1967, the situation has remained explosive, and, indeed, broke out into actual aggression when the Arabs, in 1973, caught Israel almost unprepared on the holiest day of the Jewish year — the Day of Atonement. Once again the Israelis repulsed the attack, but as yet (early 1976) there has been little sign of any true peace being achieved. The present position holds perhaps a slight promise of eventual negotiation, but the influential guerilla movements within the Arab world remain bitterly hostile.

The Jewish communities of the world rallied wholeheartedly to the support of their co-religionists in Israel, threatened with extinction, yet these events have not yet succeeded in

reconciling the conflicting elements of nationalism and
religion in the Jewish outlook. Rather have they underlined,
once again, the paradox which lies at the heart of Jewish
history.

16

THE MODERN SCENE

Where Jews are Living Today

The story of the post-biblical development of Judaism and the Jewish people has now reached its modern setting, and this concluding chapter will attempt some assessment of the Jewish role in the contemporary world. In order to present as complete and accurate a picture as possible, this must be considered in all its different aspects: social, cultural, religious, educational and demographic. For it must be borne in mind that in the Jewish ethos there is no ultimate dichotomy between religious motivation and the practical way of life (or what is called secular life), since both emanate from the same source and fountain-head. It is, for instance, impossible to separate Jewish history from Jewish religion: the two are completely interwoven.

To start with the demographic factor, the total Jewish population in the world today is somewhere between thirteen and fourteen million. Jews are widely distributed and are to be found in most countries of the world, and the following figures (based on surveys of 1969-71) give an impression of their distribution both in the main and in some of the smaller countries.

Argentine	500,000
Australia	77,000
Canada	300,000
France	550,000
Germany (inc. East & Berlin)	32,000
Great Britain	410,000
India	14,000
Iran	80,000
Israel	2,632,000
Lebanon	2,500
Morocco	35,000
Rumania	100,000

South Africa	117,990
Soviet Union	2,644,000
Syria	3,500
United States of America	6,059,000

One frequently held misconception about Jews is that they constitute a race. Indeed, the 'race myth' about so many peoples and groups today is one that does incalculable harm to human relations in general. To use the word in its scientific, biological sense, Jews belong to every branch of the human species, for there are Nordic (so-called Anglo-Saxon) types among them as well as Negroes, black Jews in India and Mongoloids in China. Most are Mediterranean in origin and appearance and resemble other Mediterranean peoples such as the Armenians. The only accurate classification is that they are a cultural group sharing a common religious and historical background.

The Social Climate

As we have seen from the historical survey in previous chapters, Jews, being a minority religious group in every country except the State of Israel, are, like other minorities, greatly affected by the general political and social climate prevailing in the different nations to which they belong. Roughly speaking, there are four distinctive environments, which may be considered as those of (a) the western democracies, (b) the totalitarian countries behind the Iron Curtain, (c) the developing countries of Asia and Africa, and (d) the predominantly Jewish environment of the State of Israel, dealt with in the last chapter.

To take first the western democracies in countries such as Great Britain, France and the United States of America (this applies also to West Germany) where cultural pluralism is recognized, Jews, like other minority denominations, have full opportunities to observe their faith and maintain their own institutions. At the same time they are integrated, at any rate legally and officially, into the national life of the country. They have, in fact, frequently played a leading part in many spheres such as the political, legal, economic, cultural

(particularly in literature, drama, music and art), and philan-
thropic. Jews have been Lord Chief Justice of England, Prime
Minister of France, and supreme commander of the
Australian army.

This does not mean that in the social sphere they are
entirely accepted or immune from prejudice: the battle for
full social integration still goes on. There have been leading
Jewish sportsmen in all countries, yet it is still difficult for
Jews in some parts of our own country to become members
of golf, tennis or cricket clubs, and they have been forced on
occasion to found clubs of their own.

There is still a Jewish 'image' in the minds of many people
which bears little relation to fact. It is often associated with
money-making and a mercenary instinct — the product of
such famous fictitious characters as Shylock in *The Merchant
of Venice* and Fagin in.*Oliver Twist*. This aspect of antisemitism is deeply rooted in people's emotions: in the envy which
takes subconscious note of hard-won successes, when a persecuted minority succeeds in carving out economic security
in a new country; in the fear (of competition, of down-
grading, of trade recession, of losing jobs and houses) which,
however irrational, takes hold of the relatively unsuccessful
majority when comparisons are drawn with the energetic
dynamism of a minority struggling to establish itself. Here,
the psychological motivation emanating from personal
anxiety, and a sense of ebbing security in a world where the
affluent society is not always evident, creates a handy scape-
goat on which to blame both inadequacy and misfortune.

There are still areas of living in which Jews, though not
prohibited, are unwelcome and often tacitly excluded. For
instance, an experiment was carried out recently by a sociologist in Canada, aimed at discovering how far anti-Jewish
prejudice still existed. He sent identical letters to selected
hotels, asking for reservations — one signed as Mr Greenberg,
the other as Mr Lockwood. To the letters with the first signa-
ture, 52 per cent of the hotels responded, of which 36 per
cent offered accommodation. To the second, where he had
signed himself 'Lockwood', 95 per cent of the hotels replied,
of which 93 per cent offered him accommodation, although,

in fact, he had written in both cases to the same hotels asking for the same dates.

Apart from the prejudice which arises because of the 'image' borne by the minority (that stereotype of 'the Jew' handed down through generations and reinforced at times of stress and change and dislocation in society) there is another aspect of antisemitism which is specifically modern. This is the plausible merging of anti-Zionism with antisemitism. It is too easy for the antisemite to argue that he has, of course, no prejudices against Jews 'as such', but that he just disagrees with Zionism. On that slippery slope, the way is only too open for a 'legitimate' antisemitism, carefully nurtured under cover of 'honest doubt' At one stroke, it inaccurately equates Judaism with Zionism, and sows the seeds of a dangerous new form of antisemitism. This is a new phenomenon, and one which is spreading. It is only fair to state, however, that opposition to Zionism on political grounds — shared by some Jews themselves — need not imply antagonism to the teaching of Judaism or the Jewish people as a whole.

A further backlash from the emergence of the State of Israel has been, again, a deeply emotional one. For centuries non-Jews have accustomed themselves to thinking of Jews as downtrodden and persecuted. Christian sympathy and support has often tended to become tinged with compassion for the under-dog, the impulse to champion the oppressed, and to see Jews only in this light, as objects of pity. Two aspects of life in modern Israel have, happily, destroyed this image, but have also created a vacuum into which, for some, a certain prejudice is creeping. One of these, of course, was the effective, independent, self-reliant pursuit of national security and independence in the Six Day War — presenting a quite different picture from the old stereotype of the crushed and humiliated Jew. The other was that earlier revelation of a young and eager people, cultivating the dry land of Israel and, literally, making the desert blossom. Here again is an aspect of Jewry which cancelled out the conventional picture of a Jew as accomplished only in trade.

Both these new lights shed on Jewry have come as a jolt to people's preconceptions and misconceptions — in some cases, a not entirely welcome jolt. There are always those who prefer the objects of their compassion to continue as tragic and rejected, or in any case as under obligation to them, and who resent any assertion of equality and independence. There is, here, a subtle emotional mechanism at work. The benefactor, whose concern springs from his own need to feel superior and who now finds himself no longer necessary, is unable to accept a radically changed relationship. He feels, in some nebulous way, let down, and his pity gives way to indignation, then critical opposition, dislike and prejudice. It is a familiar situation between individuals, or within families, and can be applied on a wider scale to relationships between groups. Not all — indeed not many — of those who have been concerned about the persecution of Jews have reacted in this fashion. But some have done so, and their rejection of success in a people who, they feel, *ought* to remain oppressed and therefore objects of concern, accounts for a certain amount of 'new' antisemitism.

In spite of evidence of this kind, however, it would be fair to say that, in the main, the struggle for freedom and human rights in the case of the Jewish and other religious minority groups has been won, and that they are reasonably well integrated into the societies of which they are members. This is, unfortunately, far from being true in the case of black minorities (or even majorities — for instance, in South Africa), but a consideration of this, perhaps the dominant problem of our day, lies outside the scope of a book on the history of Judaism. It must, however, be stressed that such prejudice and discrimination are totally opposed to both Jewish and Christian teaching, which is based on the great humanitarian principle, first enunciated in the Book of Leviticus (19.18): 'You shall love your neighbour as yourself.' It must also be stressed that prejudice is an infective disease, and that discrimination against one minority group cannot be separated from discrimination against another. In fact such infection is liable to leap across the borders which mark out one particular minority from another.

The Jewish position, however, is much less happy in

certain totalitarian countries. There, as with other religious minorities (for example, the Baptists in Soviet Russia), their situation is precarious, with special antagonism against Zionists (using the term to cover anyone who simply wants to emigrate from a country where he is not free to practise his faith openly). This means that those who want to emigrate to Israel or join their families in other countries abroad are as a rule prevented from doing so. Though religious toleration is the official policy of these totalitarian countries, and though church and synagogue services continue to a certain extent, the general atmosphere both socially and educationally is so anti-religious that Jewish communities have dwindled and in many cases disappeared. Religious teaching is prohibited in schools, and denominations are prevented from having their own educational institutions. Active oppression, though confined to individuals, is immediately countered by Jewish communities in the outside world. In Britain, for instance, demonstrations and other protests are efficiently organized by several groups working together — a form of publicity which takes advantage of the Soviet desire to win approval in the West. Though not always successful, it can be and has been an effective method when used on behalf of individuals.

With regard to Asian and African countries, the condition of the Jewish population varies in accordance with the prevailing standards of social and economic development in each particular state. Arab and Moslem countries tend to regard Jews with some hostility, owing to the emergence of the State of Israel in a land to which Arabs claim a prior right. Egyptian Jews, for example, were cruelly treated by Nasser's government after the Six Day War, while in Syria Jews suffer under crippling legislation which effectively deprives them of participation in ordinary social life — laws which are comparable with Hitler's restrictions in Nazi Germany. Generally speaking, too, in the under-developed countries where the people as a whole are culturally and materially backward, Jewish communities tend to live an impoverished and restricted life, though free to carry out their religious practice. When there has been a political upheaval, as in

Algeria, many Jewish families have migrated to other
countries, particularly, in this case, to France, since they
were French-speaking and used to the French cultural
outlook.

On the other hand, in countries controlled by the white,
westernized section of the population, such as South Africa
and Rhodesia, Jews share the prosperity of their own racial
group. Originally there was some fear that the racist policy of
nationalist South African governments might involve Jews
as well as the Bantu peoples. But this has receded of late,
though the fear of this is always just below the surface and
from time to time incidents occur which give substance to
the feeling many Jews have of walking a tight-rope.
Synagogues and Jewish cultural institutions, however,
flourish all over the Cape. This is also true, to a limited
extent, of parts of India (for example, Calcutta) and South
America. But in a country such as the Argentine there is
marked antisemitism emanating from the ultra-right-wing
Nazi groups such as Tacuara.

The Jewish Contribution to Art and Science
It is generally agreed that western art and science owe more
to ancient Greece and the Hellenic heritage than to Hebraism
and the Jewish people. This is partly due to the fear of
idolatry which was characteristic of Jewish thought and
teaching ever since prophetic times and which led,
particularly in painting and sculpture, to a firm *caveat* against
the depiction of the human form — a ruling which still
operates today among the Orthodox.

Nevertheless, Jews have made outstanding contributions
to artistic expression of every kind, though — music apart —
it is a much-disputed point as to whether this can be
classified as specifically Jewish art. Jews have tended to
produce original creative work as individuals within their
various cultural or national groups rather than as Jews.
Among authors and dramatists, there are many who have
been prominent in this country: Sir Arthur Pinero, Alfred
Sutro, Israel Zangwill, G. B. Stern, Louis Golding, Gilbert
Frankau, Naomi Jacob. Some are still remembered and all

were important in their day. Their published work is to be found in libraries, where a study of some of it would be rewarding. More recently, and with widely varying interests, we can think of Arthur Koestler, Dannie Abse, Arnold Wesker. There are many others. Looking beyond Great Britain as well as within it, we find, in the sphere of drama and dance, two enduring names — the French actresses, Rachel and Sarah Bernhardt (herself partly Jewish); our own Alicia Markova and Constance Collier, with many others; Eddie Cantor and Danny Kaye in America, the Marx Brothers, Elizabeth Bergner, and Edward G. Robinson, with such famous producers as Ernst Lubitsch, Alexander Korda and Irving Thalberg.

Music has produced a wide variety of household names, as composers, performers, and conductors: Offenbach, Meyerbeer, Bloch, Gershwin, Copland, Klemperer, the violinists Menuhin and Heifetz, the pianists Rubinstein, Kentner, Barenboim and Horowitz; while in painting and sculpture we have only to think of Epstein, Chagall, Pissarro and Modigliani.

In the fields of science and medicine, apart from the great name of Einstein, perhaps the shortest way to illustrate the involvement of Jews is to quote the caustic statement of an eminent Slav doctor, Lukatchevsky (a non-Jew), writing at the time of the Nazi promulgation of their Aryan doctrines:

Since the Jewish spirit is to be destroyed in every branch of life, according to the National Socialist doctrine, I will provide a medical guide for consistent Nazis who wish to know what to avoid when they are ill.

A Nazi who has venereal disease must not allow himself to be cured by salvarsan, because it is the discovery of the Jew, Ehrlich. He must not even take steps to find out whether he has this ugly disease, because the Wassermann reaction, which is used for the purpose, is the discovery of a Jew. A Nazi who has heart disease must not use digitalis, the medical use of which was discovered by the Jew, Ludwig Traube. If he has toothache, he will not use cocaine, or he will be benefiting by the work of a Jew, Carl

Koller. Typhoid must not be treated, or he will have to
benefit by the discoveries of the Jews, Widal and Weil. If
he has a headache he must shun pyromidon and anti-
pyrin (Spiro and Filehne). Antisemites who have convulsions must put up with them, for it was a Jew, Oscar
Liebreich, who thought of chloral hydrate. The same
with psychic ailments: Freud is the father of psycho-
analysis. Antisemitic doctors must jettison all discoveries
and improvements by the Nobel Prizemen Politzer, Barany,
Otto Warburg; the dermatologists, Jadassohn, Bruno
Bloch, Unna; the neurologists, Mendel, Oppenheim,
Kornecker, Benedikt; the lung specialist, Fraenkel; the
surgeon, Israel; the anatomist, Henle, and the others.

To revert for a moment from the sciences to the arts, and
to the doubt that there is such a thing as specifically Jewish
art, we should not forget to consider music, and particularly
the music of the synagogue. Much of this is expressed in what
is called *Hazzanut*, the cantor's chanting or intoning —
reproduced in the work of modern composers such as Bloch,
whose music may therefore be described both emotionally
and idiomatically as Jewish. There is also a considerable
amount of modern drama based on biblical and apocryphal
themes as well as the folk ways of the Hasidim (see Chap. 12)
and Jewish life in the poor quarters of industrial towns.
Examples are to be found in plays like *The Dybbuk* and the
recent work of David Kossoff. In other artistic spheres
special mention should be made of Israel Zangwill's novels
(a Jewish parallel to Dickens), and the paintings of Chagall.

Jews, of course, having been deprived for centuries of
participation in the professions which non-Jews took for
granted, were among the first to jump into specifically new
fields of activity such as the development of newspapers and
journals — a new cultural force opening up in the period of
the Emancipation — of publishing in general, and of drama,
film-production, radio and television.

What has been said about the arts applies to some extent
to the sciences. It is true that inductive, scientific research
was a product of the Hellenic genius rather than the Hebraic,

which, with its emphasis on the moral quality of life, was in ancient times little concerned with, or perhaps incapable of, free scientific inquiry and pure dialectic. Yet throughout their subsequent history extraordinary interest has been shown by Jews in mathematics, science and especially medicine. The latter derived to some extent, as we have seen in the case of Maimonides, from the deep social concern embedded in their religious teachings as well as the intellectual stimulus generated, within a limited sphere, by Talmudic and rabbinic literature — also from close association with Arabic scientists in the Golden Age of Spanish-Arabic culture. It must, surely, be more than a coincidence that the propounder of the modern theory of relativity in physics, Einstein, and the originator of psycho-analysis, Freud, were both Jews.

The Synagogue

Yet, in spite of all this intense activity, undertaken alongside non-Jewish colleagues and leading inevitably to a certain amount of integration with non-Jewish communities, religion in both synagogue and home still remains the focal point of Jewish life and identity. It is true that, where this has been thrown over as the result of conversion, intermarriage or assimilation into the general environment, the family concerned ceases in a generation or so to be Jewish. It is also true that religious observance plays a far less important part in the life of the average Jew today than it did in, say, Victorian times, and the forces of modern scepticism and materialism have had much the same effeect in breaking religious ties among Jews as among those of other faiths.

Nevertheless, there is still a vigorous synagogal and communal life in all countries where there is a Jewish population. On the two most sacred days of the year, New Year and the Day of Atonement, the synagogues are still crowded to capacity, and the religious ceremonies sanctifying birth, adulthood (*Bar Mitzvah* and *Bat Mitzvah*, see p. 16), marriage and death, still tend to be observed in most Jewish families. It is from the synagogue, too, that all kinds of educational, social, and philanthropic activities radiate, for, according to Jewish tradition, religion is essentially Halachic: it is a way of life, a total commitment and not something confined to established worship or ceremonial.

Actual worship in most synagogues today is based on Orthodox ritual, and the religious life of Orthodox Jews is still regulated by Rabbinic Courts (known as a Beth Din — 'House of Judgement') whose task it is to study and apply the directives of the *Shulhan Arukh* (see page 50). But there are, as we have seen, a large number of Reform synagogues, especially in the United States of America, where a modified ritual is in use and a number of prayers are recited in the vernacular instead of in Hebrew. There are also, as explained earlier, certain doctrinal differences between the two or more sections of the community, but all Jews are united in spirit through acceptance of the fundamental teachings of Judaism and the maintenance of a distinctive corporate and institutional life.

Religious Teaching and General Education

In what is often described as a secular age, with its scientific, materialistic outlook and a sceptical attitude towards religion and theology in general, the teaching of Judaism, as of other religions, presents considerable problems and difficulties. This is especially true with regard to communist countries where the Marxist ideology based on dialectical materialism prevails and, particularly in Soviet Russia, the Jewish community find themselves up against the strongest pressures, both social and political, when they attempt to pass on traditional religious practices and values to the rising generation. No such obstacles, however, confront the Jewish communities in western countries, at least at the official level. Here they are only faced with the apathy of so many parents in regard to religious education and practice, and partly as a consequence of this come the doubts which have arisen in young people's minds as to the truth of ancient theological beliefs. Yet it must be realized that, as has been shown in surveys carried out on this question, the vast majority of parents (over 90%) wish their children to receive religious instruction though they themselves may carry out little, if anything, in the way of religious observance. This attitude, of course, is of questionable value. It is comparable to that of the Christian who never bothers to attend church services but feels it is a correct and comforting ritual to have his children baptized and, later, married, with the full sacraments of the church — and would, indeed, be up in arms at any attempt to deprive him of what he feels to be his 'rights'. The children in such situations, whether Jewish or Christian, can only be expected to persevere with religious observances if they can see before them the infectious example of their own parents.

In most countries, Jewish children attend the ordinary state schools, and the teaching of religion is, in this situation, organized by the ecclesiastical authorities through religious schools (Hederim) or synagogue classes. Where, as in England, religious instruction and an act of worship at the morning assembly are part of the statutory school curriculum, Jewish pupils — like others belonging to minority denominations — have the right of withdrawal on grounds of conscience. There are also special schools, at both the primary and secondary stages of education, for Jewish children — the same is true for denominations of the Christian faith, such as the Roman Catholic — whose parents want them to be educated in a specifically Jewish atmosphere. These (like the church or convent schools) are as a rule recognized and partly financed by the state. In some countries, such as the United States of America, religion is divorced from the state educational system so that problems of conscience and sectional religious training do not arise.

Relations between Jews and Christians
Apart from the official and legal aspect of the question as to the sort of treatment accorded to the Jewish minorities in the various countries where they live, something must be said of the social factor, a subject already introduced in chapter 14. In recent years there has been, at least in western countries, a significant growth of religious tolerance, in what is called the ecumenical movement, deriving largely from the statements made by the World Council of Churches and the Vatican Council — the latter largely resulting from the

guidance of Pope John XXIII. This represents an attempt on the part of Christians to co-operate and find common ground with those of other faiths. There is an added bond between Jews and Christians, due to the conviction that, if they are to survive in a secular age when religious beliefs in general are so much called in question, they must make common cause and, without sacrifice of distinctive practices and belief, work together for the safeguarding of their joint Judaeo-Christian heritage, which has, throughout the last thousand years, shaped the moral structure of western civilization.

In spite of this, it cannot be maintained that all prejudice and misunderstanding between Christians and Jews has, as yet, been eliminated. On the Jewish side there are long memories of persecution by the Church, of the Crusades and the Inquisition, and of the denial of human rights in so-called Christian countries. These memories have to be eradicated, at least from their social thinking today. There still lingers, too, in some Jewish circles, partly as a result of this, partly owing to a narrow, exclusive interpretation of Judaism and the Torah, and from a fear of conversion, an unwillingness to study Christianity and the great spiritual legacy of the New Testament.

Even more serious obstacles to mutual understanding remain in some areas of Christian thinking, though, as has been said above, great efforts are being made to get rid of them. There still persists a tendency to regard the Jewish people either as a 'people accursed' for the crime of deicide, or as an obstinate group who stick to an antiquated, legalistic, tribal form of religion, and refuse to accept the Christian revelation. There is also the allegation that they are more mercenary and materialistic than other groups. These misconceptions are slowly being eliminated, partly by general education in human understanding, partly through the co-operative efforts of Church and Synagogue. It should be emphasized that, while Christians bear the great burden of a millennium's guilt in relation to persecution of the Jewish people, and while, therefore, the onus of a *rapprochement* falls largely upon the Christian community, yet Jews also — however understandable, historically, their prejudices and suspicions may be — have to overcome their own false ideas of Christians and Christianity. The new relationship has to be a mutuality rather than a one-sided attempt on the part of Christians to behave benevolently towards Jews — a fatal attitude which can never lead to true understanding.

All these ideas have been crystallized in the work being carried out by organizations composed of Christians and Jews which now exist in many western countries. In Great Britain, for instance, the Council of Christians and Jews, which now has twenty-five active branches in various parts of the country, was founded in 1942 on the initiative of a small group of people including the Revd Dr James Parkes and the Revd William W. Simpson, O.B.E. The latter was General Secretary of the Council from its inception until his retirement in 1974, and is still involved in the administration of the International Council of Christians and Jews. Largely as a result of the influence exerted by these and similar bodies, it may be said that a far better understanding now exists between Christians and Jews in western countries than at any other period in history.

The Future

The long story of post-biblical Judaism is now completed and it only remains to say a word (always a risky process) as to how it may develop in the future. What seems certain at the time of writing is that, in spite of, and perhaps because of, the new trends in scientific, economic and humanistic thought, Judaism (like Christianity and other religions) has still a vital role and will continue to survive. There are, in fact, signs of a new growth of understanding between scientists and theologians today, and a good deal of the dogmatism characteristic of the late nineteenth century has been discarded on both sides, giving place to a recognition that ultimate truth has both its spiritual and rational aspects.

It seems possible that Judaism, as in earlier Talmudic times and during the Golden Age in Spain, will show a fresh capacity for adaptation and development. It is even likely, if we are to judge from current experience, that the universalistic and humanistic elements will gain a new emphasis in the modern world, while legalistic and ceremonial aspects may undergo some modification, though here it must also be remembered that, in times of spiritual decay and confusion, the swing-back often tends to be towards a stricter orthodoxy.

Something, too, will depend on the future of the State of Israel. The threats to her existence in the Six Day War and, later, in the attack on the Day of Atonement, 1973, led to a great feeling of solidarity throughout world Jewry and a growth of nationalistic pride which is not without its dangers. There is already a conflict between the successful policy of a Jewish state, based on security and economic viability, and the higher spiritual ideals intrinsic in a Torah-rooted religion. If Israel can resolve this seeming dichotomy, she will have achieved a way of life which could be of inestimable strength and value to the West. For the problem of preserving a secular-religious balance, and the inner tension (not necessarily a destructive one) which this creates, is one which faces all peoples and all states claiming to identify themselves with a religious heritage — whether Christian, Muslim or Jewish.

Whatever the outcome, this recognition of basic human rights and the freedom of individual conscience may be said to be the fundamental principle for which the Jewish people have always stood. It is this aspect of their teaching which, if in the future they are to play a distinctive spiritual role, they are likely to emphasize more than ever in a world whose complexity and conflict cry out for satisfying answers. Jewish post-biblical history is 'history with a difference'. It is not a history like that of other peoples in which wars and politics play a dominant part. It is the record of a people believing they were chosen to bear a heavy burden: the responsibility of declaring God's laws, made known to them on Sinai, throughout the world. Its task will continue until that mission has been accomplished, and 'the earth shall be full of the knowledge of the Lord as the waters cover the sea' (Isa. 19.9).

POSTSCRIPT

There remains one particular matter to underline — the tragic question of antisemitism. Short references have appeared in various chapters, but we have consciously endeavoured to play down the sufferings of the Jewish people in a book which, we felt, should emphasize positive aspects of Jewish life rather than the dark face of their persecution.

But while enough may have been said of antisemitism as it has manifested itself in general throughout Jewish history, there is a special sense in which the Nazi destruction of European Jewry during the 1930s and early 40s has a present-day significance. For the Nazis are not merely dusty figures in an academically dry and historical past — even though, for young people today, the holocaust of six million Jews may appear totally unrelated to their own modern life. It happened, this most catastrophic outbreak of antisemitism, only forty years ago, and its effects are still making themselves felt. And if we say that the Nazis, like the poor, are always with us, this is not in any way a flippant statement, but sober truth. They come in different guises in the 1970s, and are concerned not only with Jews but with black and other minorities. They may — or may not — be German. They may — or may not — be English, Irish, French, Russian, American, South African. Take your choice.

Persecution, after all, is simply the end-product of prejudice, arrived at through active discrimination. And prejudice itself springs, always, from ignorance, from lack of compassionate understanding, and from the persecutors' blind, unreasoning fear of some unlikely threat by the persecuted — a fear which is a projection on to others of deep inner conflicts and uncertainties. It is a pre-judgement, made with emotion but without the facts. Which is why this book has been written: to offer *facts* about the way of life of a minority people who, for centuries, have been pre-judged by their neighbours. There has been ignorance. There has been a lack of compassion. There has been fear. Behind the Christian attitude has been the centuries-old charge of deicide. Without this specifically religious prejudice, Hitler could never have won support for his own basically irreligious persecution of the German and European Jews.

We need to be aware of the dangers both of religious prejudice and of its more primitive accomplice, superstition. The evil which happened during the Nazi rule in Europe left a mark upon the human spirit which has still to be recognized and with which we must come to terms — both in order that such a holocaust may never be unloosed again, and also that we may learn to know the springs of our own human conduct, however disturbing some of these may be.

But to comfort us, if, from the undoubted vantage-point of forty years on, we feel the Nazi persecution to have been the unmitigated horror which indeed it was, then we also have to remember that there were those, at the time, who thought likewise — and who knowingly paid for their resistance with their lives.

BIBLIOGRAPHY

ANTISEMITISM

The Anguish of the Jews	Edward H. Flannery (Collier-Macmillan)
Antisemitism	James Parkes (Vallentine, Mitchell)
Faith and Fratricide	Rosemary Ruether (Search Press)
The Final Solution	Gerald Reitlinger (Vallentine, Mitchell)
The History of Anti-Semitism (3 Vols)	Léon Poliakov (Routledge & Kegan Paul)
The Last of the Just (novel)	André Schwarz-Bart (Corgi Books)
The Saving Remnant	Herbert Agar (Rupert Hart-Davis)
Warrant for Genocide	Norman Cohn (Eyre & Spottiswoode)
When Compassion was a Crime	H.D. Leuner (Oswald Wolff)
While Six Million Died	Arthur D. Morse (Secker & Warburg)
The Yellow Star	Gerhard Schoenberner (Corgi Books)

HISTORY

The Course of Jewish History	Howard M. Sacher (Weidenfeld & Nicolson)
The Hebrew People	Josephine Kamm (Victor Gollancz)
A History of the Jewish People	James Parkes (Weidenfeld & Nicolson/Penguin)
Jewish Life in Modern Britain	Julius Gould & Shaul Esh (Routledge & Kegan Paul)

Mediaeval Jews	Maurice Harris (Bloch Publishing Company)
The Secret Jews	Joachim Prinz (Vallentine, Mitchell)
A Short History of the Jewish People	Cecil Roth (East & West Library)
Social History of Jews in England 1850-1950	Vivian D. Lipman (Walls & Company)
Three Centuries of Anglo-Jewish History	Vivian D. Lipman (Jewish Historical Society of England)

ISRAEL

All about Israel	Moshe Davis & Isaac Levy (Jewish National Fund)
Confrontation: the Middle East War and World Politics	Walter Laqueur (Abacus)
Encounter in Israel	Alice & Roy Eckardt (Associated Press, N.Y.)
Israel	Terence Prittie (Pall Mall Press)
The Kibbutz	Dan Leon (Pergamon Press)
Kibbutz	Melford E. Spiro (Schocken Books)
The Rift in Israel: Religious Authority and Secular Democracy	S. Clement Leslie (Routledge & Kegan Paul)
Whose Land?	James Parkes (Penguin)

JEWISH-CHRISTIAN RELATIONS

Bridge to Brotherhood	Stuart E. Rosenberg (Abelard-Schuman)
Elder and Younger Brothers	A. Roy Eckardt (Scribners)
Judaism and Christianity	Leo Baeck (Harpur Torchbooks)
Prelude to Dialogue	James Parkes (Vallentine, Mitchell)
Sweeter Than Honey	Peter Schneider (SCM Press)

We Jews and Jesus   Samuel Sandmel (O.U.P., New York)

Your People, My People   A. Roy Eckardt (New York Times Book Co.)

JUDAISM

Authorized Daily Prayer
  Book   (Eyre & Spottiswoode)

*Confrontations with
Judaism*   Philip Longworth (Anthony Blond)

*The Golden Tradition:
Jewish Life and Thought
in Eastern Europe*   Lucy Dawidowicz (Vallentine, Mitchell)

The Jewish Home   (Jewish Marriage Education Council)

Judaism   Myer Domnitz (Ward Lock Educational)

Judaism   Isidore Epstein (Penguin)

Judaism   Leo Trepp (Dickenson Publishing Co., Calif.)

Judaism as Creed and Life   Morris Joseph (Routledge)

Light and Rejoicing   William W. Simpson (Christian Journals Ltd., Belfast)

Judaism: a Portrait   Cecil Roth (Faber & Faber)

Outlines of Liberal Judaism   C.G. Montefiore (Macmillan)

Reform Judaism   Ed: Dow Marmur (Reform Synagogues of Great Britain)

The Story of Judaism   Bernard J. Bamberger (Schocken)

Two Types of Faith   Martin Buber (Routledge & Kegan Paul)

Understanding Jews   Stuart E. Rosenberg (Hodder & Stoughton)

*Understanding Your Jewish
Neighbour*   Myer Domnitz (Lutterworth Educational)

RABBINICS AND MYSTICISM

A Guide to Hassidism	M. Rabinovicz (Thomas Yoseloff)
Rabbinic Theology	Solomon Schechter (Schocken Books)
Rabbinic Theology	Roy A. Stewart (Oliver & Boyd)
The World of the Talmud	Morris Adler (Schocken)
Zohar, the Book of Splendour	Gershon G. Scholem (Schocken)

PAMPHLETS

There are various organizations which specialize in booklets and pamphlets, also films or filmstrips, and which will generally provide speakers for discussion groups or other meetings:

1 The Central Jewish Lecture Committee
   Board of Deputies of British Jews
   Woburn House
   Upper Woburn Place
   London WC1H OEP

2 The Council of Christians and Jews
   48 Onslow Gardens
   London SW7 3PX

   The Council publishes a wide range of relevant pamphlets, as well as a quarterly journal, *Common Ground*. It has also a comprehensive library.

3 Jewish Information Service
   Reform Synagogues of Great Britain
   34 Upper Berkeley Street
   London W1H 7PG

4 The Jewish National Fund (material on Israel)
   Rex House
   4-12 Regent Street
   London SW1

5 The Study Centre for Christian Jewish Relations
   17 Chepstow Villas
   London W11 3DZ

Star Struck